DRAWING BOOK.

Frontispiece.

A PROGRESSIVE

DRAWING BOOK.

FOR BEGINNERS.

By PHILIP H. DELAMOTTE, F.S.A.

PROFESSOR OF DRAWING IN KING'S COLLEGE AND SCHOOL, LONDON.

"It has pleased the Designer of 'the world and all that therein is,' not only to surround man with the ever-varying and inexhaustible beauties of nature, and to endow him with the gift of sight to perceive her graces; but he has been pleased also to confer upon him a mind to understand, and a hand to imitate them."

M. DIGBY WYATT.

London:

MACMILLAN AND CO.

1869.

[*The Right of Translation and Reproduction is reserved.*]

LONDON:
R. CLAY, SONS, AND TAYLOR, PRINTERS,
BREAD STREET HILL.

PREFACE.

THE following work is intended to give such instructions to Beginners in Drawing, and to place
before them copies so easy, that they may not find
any obstacle in making, what is the principal difficulty in every undertaking, the first step. Thence-
forward, the lessons are gradually progressive. By
reading carefully the instructions, and then copying
to the best of his ability the Drawings here placed
before him, the student, whatever may be his age,
will meet with no difficulty that he cannot overcome by a little patience. After this course, instead
of being bewildered with the complications of large
drawings, through the instrumentality of these simple
copies he will learn, beneath the seeming confusion
of larger subjects, to trace the principal design, to
seize the salient points, to add by degrees the details,
and in the end to finish accurately what formerly he
could not have attempted. As he advances, each

line will have a meaning to him, and it will no longer be necessary to cover patches of paper with unmeaning shades, in order to hide deficiencies.

Works with the same intention as this have been offered to the Art student before, but they have not accomplished all that might have been done. It is hoped that experience and time have, in Drawing as in other branches of education, taught the Teachers to be more explanatory, to see more clearly the difficulties of their pupils, and to shorten the modes in which these difficulties may be overcome. Mechanical improvements, too, have lent their aid. The whole of the plates have been engraved by a new process, by means of which a varying depth of tone—up to the present time the distinguishing characteristic of pencil drawing—has been imparted to woodcuts. For this process I am indebted to Mr. J. D. Cooper, whose care in executing the drawings with fidelity and accuracy cannot be too highly praised.

P. H. D.

King's College, 1869.

CONTENTS.

DRAWING BOOK.

Drawing Materials, and how to use them.— The materials necessary for elementary drawing are neither numerous nor expensive. The subjoined list will be found to comprise all that are absolutely required in order to follow the instructions in the accompanying lessons; and it will be a long time before the beginner will find that he is able profitably to make use of more.

LIST OF MATERIALS.

Some sheets of drawing paper.
A plain drawing board, and a dozen pins.
A small **T** square.
A pair of pencil bows or compasses.
India-rubber, or other eraser.
HB, B, and BB pencils.

B

Drawing Paper. — This should be white and unglazed. White paper is preferable in the earlier stages, because corrections can be made either with bread or india-rubber without any great injury to the surface or colour of the paper ; whereas, with tinted paper, the surface is liable to be removed by the action of the eraser, and a different shade lying below is then exposed. Unglazed paper also allows a greater variety of tint. It is impossible to get a deep transparent shade upon a highly-glazed surface. Either ordinary cartridge paper, or Whatman's medium, answers the purpose extremely well, and these, as well as all other necessary materials, can be procured of any artists' colourman.

The Drawing Board and Drawing Pins.—The drawing board should be flat, smooth, and so made with cross pieces that it will not warp or curve. Mahogany is, of course, more durable ; but a plain deal board has a softer and pleasanter touch. The common flat-headed pins hold down the paper without tearing it at the corners, and they allow the hand, arm, and T square to work over them without inconvenience. The paper should be placed on the board quite flat, having its edges parallel to its sides ; it should then be fastened down with as few pins as will hold it firmly in its position, so as to leave an opportunity of using the T square freely, to indicate the upright and horizontal lines. Care should be taken to keep the paper perfectly flat whilst fastening it. Paper put on slovenly, at all kinds of angles to the board, or with bulging corners, is very apt to lead the eye astray, and to cause false shadows and inequalities of tone.

Attention to these minor matters may seem to be of slight consequence, but everything that contributes to neatness and accuracy adds to the value of the work done, and helps to the acquirement of good habits. At a later period of his career, the artist may have to contend against all kinds of difficulties, and he shows himself deficient either in courage or skill if he shirks them ; but the student, until he has acquired the skill, should never, so far as he can avoid it, create difficulties for himself.

The T Square.—The square will be found of great service, especially to the beginner, as it gives him the power of ruling at least one straight line, either perpendicular or horizontal, by which he may guide his eye and hand to determine whatever else may depend on these lines. These ruled lines should be drawn lightly and delicately, with sufficient firmness to be easily seen during the progress of the work, but at the same time light enough to be rubbed out with facility when the outline is completed.

The Pencil Bows.—In some of the copies (as in Lessons 5, 6, 7, and 11) will be found a light circle or part of a circle, intended, like the straight line mentioned above, to guide the eye in keeping the general outline correct. The circle will be conveniently drawn by means of the pencil bows, and these can be occasionally used also for the measurement of lines. It will be generally found that a slip of paper, or even the pencil itself, will be a more ready instrument for measuring the length of a line, or the position of a point; but it will be better to avoid, as much as possible, reliance upon measurement. The direction of lines, the extent of an angle, the accidental combinations of lines and figures, all afford means of determining distances which, as they are also to be found in nature, may be made available when in future studies we have got beyond either compasses or slips of paper. By avoiding a reliance on measurement at first, a serious impediment to future progress is avoided.

Erasers.—For the purpose of correcting lines that have been wrongly drawn, for obliterating the guiding lines, and for keeping the paper free from unnecessary marks, it will be found necessary to use stale bread or india-rubber. The former of these is in most cases preferable, as it does no injury to the surface of the paper, but occasionally a line which will not yield to its influence can be removed by the india-rubber. The harder forms of this substance should not be used. In all cases in which it is possible to avoid erasure it is better to do so, both because the drawing thus retains a freshness it can never regain when it has once been marked, and because it encourages an attempt at accuracy at first, and, in consequence, a con-fidence in the draughtsman, which in time leads to really firm and truthful work. The superfluous lines can frequently be turned to account in shading or other ways.

Pencils.—For all ordinary outlines HB pencils should be used. The B and BB come in useful for shading. Care should be taken to have good points to the pencils, as it is impossible to have clean, accurate, and neat work with a slovenly point. With a pencil cut as in fig. B (only too accurate a sketch of many a beginner's attempt), it is impossible to see where one is making a mark: the wood hides the lead from the eye; and again, any part of the broad expanse of lead may be leaving its trail upon the paper, when it is the in-

tention of the draughtsman only to make one thin delicate line. The wood and lead should alike be cut straight and firmly *away* from the operator, who by this means keeps his hands unsoiled by the plumbago, for a process which of all others requires neatness and cleanliness. The

Fig. A.   Fig. B.

habit of cutting pencils in this way can soon be acquired, the main thing being to have a sharp knife, and to cut boldly enough at the proper angle. The pencils at the present day are so well made that they do not readily break under careful management.

Position of the Hand.—Great attention must be paid to the way in which the pencil is held. Most people know how to hold the hand in writing, the importance of a proper position being enforced at an early age. The position of the hand in draw-ing is even more im-portant than in writing, and it is very different. In writing it is only re-quisite to make lines of moderate lengths, in most cases straight, and almost always at one particular angle. In drawing every variety of length, of curve, and of angle is required, as well as an ever-varying depth of stroke. Great freedom, power, and de-licacy, then, are wanted. In sketching with char-coal, or drawing in pen-cil a large subject with

Fig. C.

flowing lines, the implement should be held lightly as in fig. C. The whole arm is then free to follow the motions of the hand, and the curves can be made

by means of any or all of the numerous joints between the shoulder and the tips of the fingers.
Mathematical curves of the greatest complexity, as
well as curves which have never yet been reduced
to mathematical expression, can be traced by this

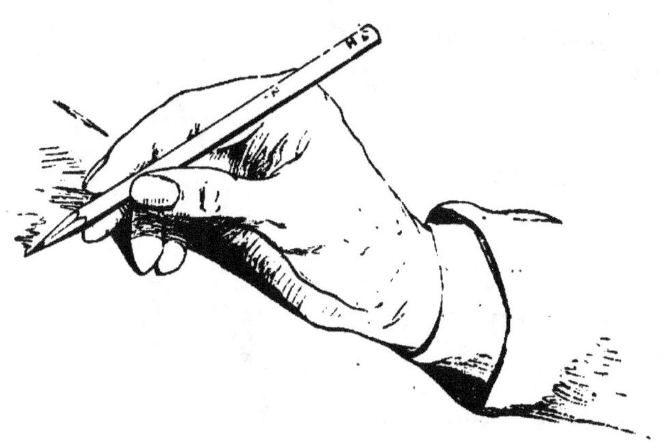

Fig. D.

delicate natural instrument with an accuracy which
it were useless to attempt by machinery.

When, however, the first general outline is sketched,
and it becomes necessary to go over the whole again
with a firmer touch, another position, such as is
shown in fig. D, is to be adopted. The arm, almost
to the elbow, should rest on the board or table, and
the wrist should be slightly raised still to give

freedom, unless a very minute and firm short line has to be drawn, then the side of the palm may rest on the paper; but on no account should a cramped, unnatural position, such as is shown in fig. E, be adopted. The pencil should be held between the

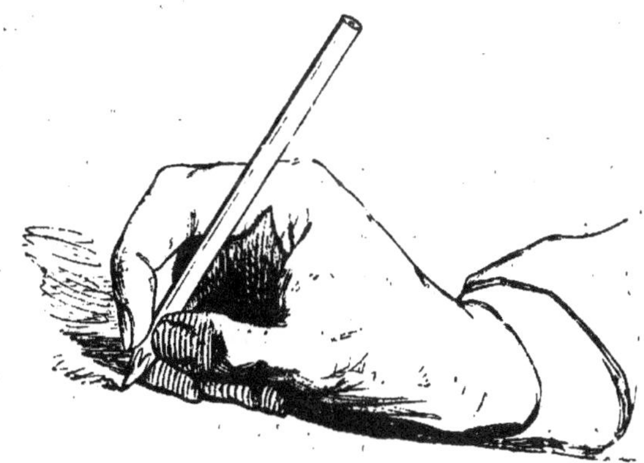

Fig. E.

pads of the fingers and thumb, not at all by the ends of them; and though the draughtsman should have perfect command over his instrument, it must be held lightly, and not grasped as in a vice. The fingers should not come too near the point; and at times, when long flowing lines are required, a position some way up the pencil will be found best.

Shading.—When the student can draw an outline

tolerably correctly, the next point is to gain some knowledge of shading. A perfect understanding of the mode of shading is all-important, because outlines denote the shape of the external figure only, whereas true and faithful shading ought to clearly define the shape of all within the outline. In the example given on Plate F the outline of the sphere is simply a circle —difficult enough to draw no doubt, still neither of so much consequence in a picture, nor requiring so much attention as the amount of shading within that out-line. The surfaces that have to be represented by shading are either comparatively flat or decidedly curved. According to the character of the surface the style of shading must be of the kind indicated in figs. 1, 2, 3, and 7, or in figs. 4, 5, 6, and 8. Fig. 1 shows how shading should be commenced— with steady even strokes, parallel to one another, and at equal distances. These should be crossed by similar lines at an obtuse angle. The result is a tolerably even dark surface, with light spots of a diamond shape at regular distances. The effect of this is an even tint having a certain amount of bright-ness. It will be good practice to accustom the hand to make these lines with pen, pencil, or chalk at odd moments. A sheet of waste paper, covered with even,

parallel lines, will be found useful ; for neatness and
accuracy in work of this kind can only be acquired
by extensive practice. When the tint is not dark
enough by these simple crossed lines (called cross-
hatching), a third set of lines at an angle between the
other two, as in fig. 2, should be added. This may
be supplemented again by others at right angles to
the last, as in fig. 3, and finally lines at all kinds
of angles, as in fig. 7, may be worked in. But in all
cases, except perhaps the last, and even in this transparency is better preserved by avoiding the practice,
care should be taken not to make any back strokes
with the pencil. The lines made in one direction
will have one depth, whilst those made in the return
of the pencil will be lighter ; these will fill up the light
spots left between the lines with a light tint, and will
hinder both the transparency and the depth of the
shade. When the pupil has accustomed himself to
make the requisite varieties of shade by various
modifications of these four figures—sometimes making
short deep strokes, and only crossing them once or
twice, at others making longer, thicker, and lighter
marks, crossing them frequently and so obliterating
all trace of the working, and only leaving a clear,
delicate, but light tone—he may attempt the curved

lines given in the lower group, following the same process as with the straight lines, beginning with one set crossed by one other, then adding a third at an intermediate angle, but the fourth should not be as with the straight lines, at right angles, but at a more moderate slope, as the bottom lines in fig. 6. In fig. 8, which represents the character of pencil drawing very accurately, almost every variety of curve is to be found.

Now for the application of these modes of shading to actual figures. A sphere has been chosen, because it is the simplest of all curved surfaces, and it is therefore a type of others in which more complicated curves occur. The process to be used is the one indicated by nature. If when the student has this copy before him he will also place a ball at a little distance* in front of h:m, so that the light falls on the left hand side of it, and rather on the upper part (a plain hollow india-rubber ball will do as well as anything, the dull drab colour not reflecting the light too strongly), the first thing he will notice will

---

* In placing objects from which to draw, it is well to have the light on the left, in order that the shadow of the hand may not interfere with the work. At the same time the direct sunlight causes too distinct shadows to be pleasant. The dispersed light from *one* window not exposed to the sun will be found far less puzzling to the beginner.

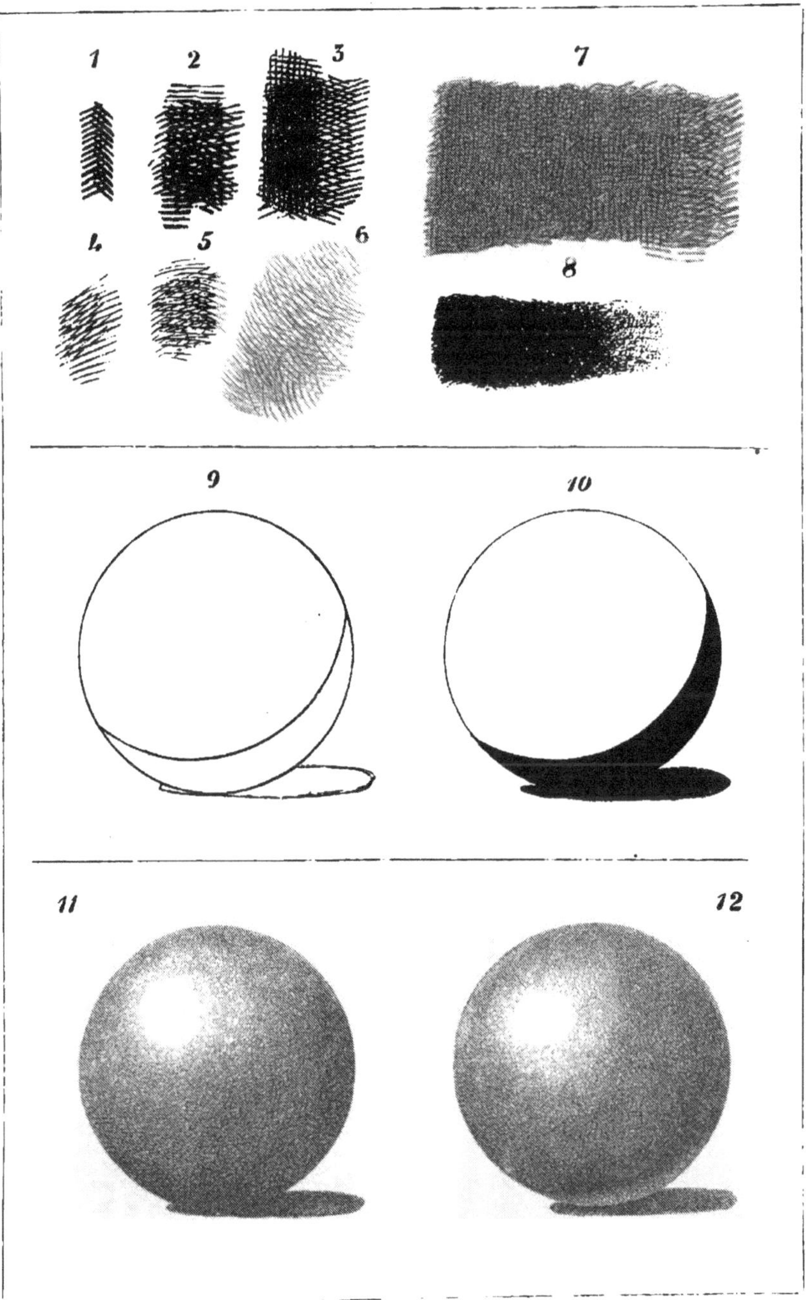

be the shade and shadow outlined in fig. 9, and put into almost full depth in fig. 10. He will then per-
ceive that this shade is graduated off to the light spot on the left. This he should leave a little too large, as it will be easy to reduce it, but impossible to recover it if once lost. If he does this accurately, his drawing should look something like fig. 11. Then on looking at the ball more carefully, he will perceive there is a little reflected light immediately above the sha-

Fig. G.

dow. This he will be able to produce by deepening the shade on the sphere a little way from the edge, and easing this shade off towards the light spot. A careful study a few times repeated of the copy, and then from the ball itself, varied by some figure not quite so regular as a ball, such as a piece of unglazed earthenware, or a plaster of Paris cast of very simple form, will not only practise the student in shading, but will accustom his eye to discover where the shade really falls, and where reflected lights may be expected.

Such practice as this is an excellent preparation for drawing from natural objects like that given in fig. G.

DESCRIPTION OF THE PLATES.

BEFORE attempting to copy any of the drawings in this book, the student will do well to read carefully through the corresponding lesson given below; and afterwards, when he has done his work, and feels fairly satisfied with it, he should again read these remarks, in order that he may see wherein he has failed, and how he might have avoided some of the difficulties he may have met with.

The earlier lessons commence with the very simplest lines, going on gradually to others at various angles, then to simple curves, and to the natural shapes to be found in leaves, &c. It will be well if at first a perpendicular line is ruled down the centre of the paper as a guide to the eye and hand until the student is able to make an upright line by hand; but he should accustom himself to rely less and less upon such aid, and finally to do without it altogether. This remark may apply also to most of the dotted

lines given in the plates: at first they may be ruled
or marked out with compasses, afterwards they
should be slightly sketched out by hand, and finally
they should be omitted altogether, being simply
used as guides to the eye, without being indicated
on the paper. It will be advisable too for beginners
to draw all these copies, both the size given in
the copy, and afterwards twice that size, partly on
account of the boldness and confidence this plan will
give to the style, and partly to accustom the eye
to enlarge or diminish a given subject without dis-
proportion.

THE LESSONS.

Lesson 1.—Let the student begin by drawing the upright stroke *a b* firmly, distinctly, and evenly. He should then make the horizontal lines *a c* and *d e*, beginning at *a* and *d*. After that he may start from *c* for *d*, taking care to keep the required angle by determining, before he commences, where *c* should be, and going directly to the already indicated point *d*, and not altering the locality of *d* afterwards to suit the direction of *c d*. Then he may erect the perpendicular *f g*. After drawing the three horizontal lines, he should begin at *h* in order to make the line *h i*, and, without altering the position of the paper, he should try and draw *h j* at the same angle in the opposite direction, concluding with the upright lines, which should be kept at the height corresponding to the lines above them.

Lesson 2—In this copy the student should first attempt the square 1 2 3 4, beginning with 1 2, then drawing 1 4 and 2 3 of equal length (which length will be marked off by the light line from 1 to 3), and the line from 4 to 3. The direction of lines 1 2, 4 3, and 2 3 should then be followed for equal distances, the light line again helping to indicate the distance, and the concluding lines will naturally fall into their places.

In the centre figure the squares should first be drawn in the same way as those above, the curved lines 5 6 and 5 7 may then be attempted, care being taken to make them both correspond.

In the lowest figure, when the oblong has been sketched, the upper line must be accurately divided in half, whilst the lower should be cut in four, thus the points where the curved lines touch the straight lines will be determined. The lower curve being then drawn, it will afford an indication of where the upper one is to come. In each of these figures, when the outline has been satisfactorily sketched, it will be better to go over the whole again, so as to make the lines of even depth and breadth throughout.

Lesson 3.—Before beginning this copy, the student should study the proportions and angles in the drawing, otherwise he will be almost sure to show too much of the top of the cube. It will be well to draw a light line as indicated by the dotted line in the copy, and above this to raise the lines to A and B at their respective angles. Attention to these angles will greatly assist the beginner in determining the right proportions of the figure. When these lines are determined, it will be easy to draw the lines at the back of the top, by noticing the direction of the opposite corners, and then to let fall the perpendiculars, to make them the same lengths, and finally to draw the bottom lines parallel to the top.

In copying the lower figure, after following the directions given in the preceding paragraph as regards the angles and outlines, care should be given to a kind of expression which has not been attempted before—viz., the depth of each line. They are in this case not all equally black, but there is a regular gradation from the foremost and firmest to the lightest at the most distant corner.

Lesson 4.—A light line had better be drawn at first from A to B with the **T** square, and properly divided. The height of the curves should then be determined by a dot, and the curves themselves marked out very lightly; the different parts must be made to correspond; and when it is satisfactorily sketched out, it should all be gone over firmly, making the line of even tone and width throughout. Similarly, the line C D should be given as lightly as possible—it being intended simply to guide the eye as to points or curves that fall under one another, and to show the deflexion of each side.

Lesson 5.—The next few copies are drawings of natural leaves, and these take a great variety of very beautiful shapes. Notice the light circles given as guides to form and size. Begin in each case with the upright line in the middle of the leaf, and branch off on either side to an equal distance, and at equal angles. Of course the curves here given very lightly do not occur in nature, but the eye should be trained to look for, and imagine them as helps to a just proportion. In copying, these imaginary lines should be done as lightly as possible, so as to give an opportunity of erasing them afterwards.

Lesson 6.—In doing the ivy leaf, the circle is the first thing ; then the upright central line from a little below the real centre of the circle comes next, to which may be added the lines down the middle of the side leaflets ; and then the outlines, taking care in each case to keep the proper depth of line after the first light sketch is made. In no case should the outline be made at first darker than the lightest portion of it ; but when the whole is got in and corrected, go over it again, putting in the proper depth for each part. In the passion-flower leaf the line *a b* will be the first ; then the sides of the leaflet to which it belongs, and the other leaflets in the same order.

Lesson 7.—The same kind of subject is here continued. Notice now the double line down the middle of the oak leaf, and the varied thickness of the line round the edge. The curved dotted line round the ground-ivy leaf should be carefully copied before the outline is attempted. In each of the leaves of this and of the other copies, the lines on the one side are thin and light, on the other thick and decided.

Lesson 8.—In the leaf of the black bryony, the student should notice how the curved markings inside the leaf gradually change from nearly the shape of the outline whilst near it, to an approach to the straight central line as they tend towards the latter.

Lesson 9.—The same remarks that have been made before, will apply to these copies, which are only more complicated forms, requiring, in consequence, more care ; but the mode of execution is the same as in the preceding examples.

Lesson 10.—Here we have more difficulty, owing to the irregularity of the outline, and the difference of position of the garlic leaves. In the upper one the central line will still guide us considerably— if we notice that the curve is continued in the same line as the stalk. This will give a starting-point from which we may be able to lead the various curves of outline of the lower edge. The line here is bold and decided ; above it is light and delicate. In the lower of the garlic leaves, too, the central line will be the starting one, with reference to which the outer edge will approach or depart ; and in this seeming irregularity there is an agreement between the two sides. When the upper side bulges higher, the lower approaches the central line, and the reverse.

Lesson 11.—In the flowers given in this copy, the circles and dividing lines marked in the upper row suggest how accuracy may be obtained in other specimens. The markings of the leaves themselves are some considerable assistance. A slight attempt at shading now appears. In this, keep the strokes in the direction given in the copy, which it will be observed is that of the texture of the leaf. Each stroke is distinct, light, and broad, made with a lightly held pencil, the point of which has been worn down. These strokes should be made at one even movement, and not by a series of hard, scratchy lines. Notice in the violet how the shading follows the direction of each petal, so as to be at five different angles.

Lesson 12.—The flowers in this plate present some irregularities, and the outline is purposely broken in places. The lines of the shading follow to a great extent the direction of the texture of the leaf; but as the shading is narrow, it is made up of short lines. One or two longer lines in the contrary direction would not have the same effect.

Lesson 13.—We now proceed to more complicated figures, and to lines of a great variety of curvature. As before, the central lines of the petals in the Iris flower, and of the leaflets in the vine leaf, will guide the eye to the true direction of the curves, and in the lower figure the indentations of the leaf must be done after the general direction of the curves has been marked out.

Lesson 14.—The spray of holly leaves and berries forms an example full of most beautiful and varied curves, no two of which are alike. In the berries, when the outside circle is completed, put the little

 DRAWING BOOK.

dot as given in the copy, and note the indication of shape which it immediately gives. There is a slight amount of shade in a single light broad line on one side of most of these berries. The student will do well to draw this copy two or three times.

Lesson 15.—The horned poppy leaf here given affords a good illustration of the plan hitherto pursued of drawing the central line first. Complicated and confused as the outline appears at first sight, it is reduced to order and regularity when compared with this line; the lower indentations advancing to gradually diminishing distances from it as you proceed from left to right (the easiest direction to draw the curve), and the points in like manner advancing further from it.

In the crocus remember that the portions of the leaves above and below the flower are in the same line.

Lesson 16.—Here we get something more of the full form of a plant. The central line of the leaves is not present to guide us, but the curve is simple, and the petals have the line slightly marked. The general shape of the poppy flower should be sketched before each petal is drawn. Again notice the direction of the small amount of shadings, and the difference of tone on the sides of the stalk. These flowers should be carefully studied, as the curves are long and sweeping, and require considerable boldness in execution. It will be found that they will be more easily accomplished if the arm be well rested and the hand allowed to move freely on the wrist.

Lesson 17.—The drawing of the Iris will require care from its irregularity. Notice should be here taken how the simple form of the lines, not having long sweeping curves, but being sharp and angular, give a notion of great strength and solidity. In copies of this character the value of various kinds of line may be well studied.

Lesson 18.—In this case the flowers and leaves are foreshortened, and thus the curves will not only require care, but the student, by asking himself why the lines run in this way, will be acquiring a knowledge of the art by which he may be hereafter enabled to copy from nature itself similar forms. Care again must be taken about the force of the lines and the directions of the shading. The depth and force of many of the outlines occasionally serve instead of shading, and give all the appearance of roundness and solidity to the petals.

Lesson 19.—Compare the berries in this copy with those of the holly in Lesson 14. See how the additional shading gives increased roundness. Now, too, the texture of the stems is marked by lines in various directions, some crossing the others, and of various depths. The seemingly scratchy and tentative strokes all have a purpose, and should be copied exactly.

Lesson 20.—Note how the shade on the petal, pointing downwards gradually though not regularly, increases in tone. The crossed lines (called henceforth cross-hatching) on the upper part of the stem, give both shade and colour. They are at the same time a preparatory exercise on what we shall have a good deal to say presently. The strokes here, as in so many of these later drawings, are to be made at once with a pencil whose point ought to be purposely worn down until the lead has become broad enough to make the line at one effort. A repetition of lines with a fine-pointed pencil will not have by any means the same effect.

Lesson 21.—Here again we have an indication of great strength, owing to the short angular lines. The flower itself exhibits this apparent strength; but tear it to pieces, and you will see that the petals are no firmer than others which do not indicate a like solidity of form.

Lesson 22.—We must now return to what was said above (page 10) about shading. Shading does for the internal form what the outline does for the external. If a person stands with the profile towards us, a fair likeness may be made by a mere outline, because it indicates the projection and depression of nose, mouth, chin, &c. ; but if we have the full face presented to us, the outline no longer accomplishes this : we require something which will suggest the amount of relief in which the various features stand. Now, shading does this in the human face, and it does this moreover for all those surfaces which, though not so distinctly marked to our observation with indentations and irregularities, have a character of their own impressed upon them by their individual peculiarities of form. Shading then is one of the great means of indicating form, and as such it must be carefully and *lovingly* studied by a beginner. The page before us should be copied again and again, till the meaning of each line is fully understood. It will be noticed that the specimens given at the top of the page are not composed of such straight or regular lines as those used in the shading of the cube in Plate F, but they give more indication of texture, more play of incidental lights and shade, more notion of that variety of nature which art can only suggest, and not fully imitate. Then see how this style of shading is used in denoting the solidity and peculiar cleavage of the different blocks of stone given below, the dark patch of sky behind the lighter stone, the shadow on the uneven ground, and even the leafage of the grass, which of course cannot be strictly copied from nature. In the adaptation of various kinds of line—thin hard lines, broad soft ones, dark and light, with all their innumerable gradations and combinations—lies the great secret of effective and true pencil drawing. Too much practice then cannot be given to this important subject. The little piece of zig-zag line which so clearly indicates rough grass, should be copied over and over again, not with a view to catch a mannerism, but to obtain a power of forming a certain class of line which will help towards expressing your thoughts, though it will not supply the place of the thought.

Lesson 23.—Here we have no longer the curves and angles of nature, but in this copy we attempt a work of art, homely art though it be, the art of the potter's wheel. Notice that the lines which denote the sides of the jar could not be marked off with a rule. They must be upright, and for this uprightness we must trust to the eye, with perhaps a guiding line from the side of the paper, or, if need be, from the **T** square. But the lines must not be ruled, they must be drawn by hand, they must be of various depths, and at places they must break off; thus they will give a far better notion of solidity and roughness of material than any ruled lines could do. The best plan perhaps to convince a learner in these matters is experience; therefore try ruling a copy as well as drawing one, and compare its different effect. In copying the brown paper cover, mark how the sharp lines indicate the stiffness of the paper. The shading stopping before it comes to the edge shows a crease. The marking of the string gives all the shade required for that. Practise the gradual lightening of the shade down (*not quite the edge*, but) the side of the jar.

Lesson 24.—Two positions of an old portmanteau. The darkening of one line in the top corner betrays a rent. The shade beneath the cover throws it off from the body, and lets one see that it is far from tightly closed. The outline of what would be a better-shaped box has been left, in order to show how we may get the irregularities by first drawing the regularities. In the same way a portion of the handle, which is not really in sight, is left, that the learner may see how he may get his outline correct, by adding sometimes the full form of a thing, a portion of which is out of sight. In the lower drawing, though no such lines are given, the student will find that he will get the curve and irregularity of the top more exactly if he first draw a light line where it ought to go. Beginners are very apt to draw things as they think they ought to be : now these attempts may be made very useful if they will afterwards look over and *criticise* their own drawings, starting from where the lines ought to be, and getting, probably after one or two failures, at where they really are. So in the copy before us : if the lines, as they ought to be, are slightly sketched, then the deflexion from them made, a tolerably exact copy will be the result.

Lesson 25.—A rush-bottomed chair, such as is often met with in churches. The planed, sharp-edged top and cross-bars are denoted by very different lines from those used to indicate the rounded legs, or the soft and flattened rushes or flags. Each leg too has its appropriate depth of tone according to its distance from the spectator : the nearest most strongly and firmly pencilled, the furthest being the lightest. As these two latter come immediately in contact, this difference can be most clearly seen. The little flaws in the wood give a character to the legs on which they occur.

Lesson 26.—In the case of the book and roll of this lesson, the rules already given should be again observed. The line A B is nearly straight, *not quite*— notice the irregularity ; this, with the stroke of shade below it, reveals an indentation in the roll. This line will give the direction of the lower line of the roll, which is only partially seen, and so too will give a clue to the direction of the line of the piece folded back. And so the line C D shows the direction the upper line of the book will necessarily take, and, with a certain amount of deviation, the lowest line of the paper or parchment. The clasps squeeze in the old volume sufficiently to make up for the retirement of the back, so that both back and front are of the same depth. A newer volume in the background is marked with sharper lines. The graduation of the shade to the point C is a good study.

Lesson 27.—The foremost of the pans here portrayed should be attempted first, because the whole of it is visible. Mark the top and bottom points of the circular opening (not circular in the picture by any manner of means); either draw a light line between them or imagine it—and an artist ought to be able to see a whole picture on a sheet of blank paper—then determine the points at the bottom of the sockets for the handles at equal distances from this line. The line joining these will not be at right angles to the former line. Then measure the distance you have determined on your drawing, and the distance in the copy, and see how much less the latter is than you had imagined. These four points being fixed, remember that the lines of the curve pass through these points at right angles to the lines you have drawn or imagined. Making short lines to pass through these points, a great portion of the work is over; the lines have only now to be coaxed into bending towards one another, and if this is done evenly, the outline is completed. In going on with the further pan, the same process must be pursued, even so far that the whole upper rim must be sketched in, in order to make sure of an even curve; the rise in a portion of it being of course neglected at first.

The bottoms will easily follow the curve of the upper rims. The handle of the foremost pan will be more easily managed by noting where its central point should come, and where it crosses the lines already drawn. This copy will repay careful study, and it may well be drawn again and again.

Lesson 28.—Much the same principles as those proposed in the last lesson should guide the student in this copy. The lower part of the flask is not a circle, and therefore the lines across will not be sufficient indication. But four points taken where the cord joins the flask at the top, and where the *quasi* foot meets the curve at the bottom, give clues to the various curves we require. Besides this, the width of the bottle at the widest part shows exactly how much curvature is required. Points should be taken thus:

and the curvature is obtained without difficulty ; and when the sides of the flask are delineated, the same process will give the band stretching down the vessel.

This done, the transverse bands may be *lightly* indicated, even across the upright band if it is found convenient, as the shading will conceal the strokes. It must be noticed that these lines are not all parallel; the upper ones have scarcely any curvature, the lower ones curve almost as much as the foot, and the intervening ones advance through all the intermediate stages. When all is sketched in lightly, note the various depths of each of these lines indicating the transverse bands. Each has a dark beginning beneath the upright flat piece; it gets lighter to about two-thirds of the way, then darkens again; disappears beneath the upright ribbon, and reappears at its darkest, getting lighter again as it approaches the edge. Each of these insignificant lines, as they seem, passes through all these stages, and the student who would fairly copy this drawing must keep this series in his mind as he goes through what he might otherwise esteem it, the drudgery of this portion of his work.

Lesson 29.—A different view of the same subject is frequently useful practice, because, while some of the work is easy from the previous exercise, so there are sure to be some new difficulties which will receive all the greater attention. Here the main circles must be first determined in the manner described in Lesson 27, by lines drawn across them, in this case at right angles ; and in both circles, viz. the outer line of the flask and the edge of the foot, the complete and even circle should first be lightly indicated, and the deviations from regularity made afterwards. The bands down the plaiting can next be put in, the requisite curve being given by the three points, and then the inner portions of circles can be carried from the one band to the other. The depth of each line should be carefully remembered as in the last copy, during the process of deepening the strokes, and the shading given at last to complete the roundness which is already beginning to be felt.

Lesson 30.—What a beautiful and delicate subject do these feathers make, and at first sight how difficult does it appear to imitate anything like the delicacy of nature ; but by following out the principles already inculcated, and by a little care and patience, the student will find that he will approach much more nearly to a satisfactory result than he could in any way have anticipated. In the first place, to begin with the upper figure, the main curve of the central line, and the general line of the outer edges, will be the starting points from which all the rest may be worked up by degrees. Next the irregularities and breaks of the edges, and the lines leading up to them from the central quill, will fall naturally into their places ; afterwards the outline of the natural markings of the feather, then the shading and working in of these markings, and at last a few strokes to indicate the direction of the featherings, will complete the main portion of the feather. The single lines which represent individual fibres of the downy part, must be left to the finishing, when also the shadow beneath will be put in.

In the lower portion showing another piece of plumage, the same process must be observed : the outline of the part that is away must be kept firmly in the mind, or lightly on the paper, and the individual markings reserved until the larger curves are determined ; then, the direction being fixed on, the pencil will readily execute the required stroke, and leave the proper depth of shading at the same time.

Lesson 31.—We now return to natural objects and delicate curves. The human mouth, as seen in the two sets of copies 31 and 32, presents an immense variety of expression and of character. It may be taken at any angle, and it requires a thorough study of form in order to denote the character we wish at a given angle. It will be found that the profiles are the easiest. Here must be noticed first the line at which the edges of the lips overhang one another, then how far back the mouth extends, the varying curves of both lips, the much lighter line where the lip joins the face,—scarcely in fact discernible, compared with the dark outline elsewhere. The tendency of the corners of the mouth upwards or downwards makes all the difference between sorrow and pleasure.

Lesson 32.—The same remarks that have been made before apply here. None of the lines in this copy must be too dark. They do not indicate any great amount of shade, only the outline of the feature itself. Notice the sweeping curves of the eyes, very different from those of the mouth; and though each one approaches the one nearest to it, no two have the same direction entirely. The eyeball is slightly shaded, but the shade ends before we come to the edge, leaving the reflected light.

Lesson 33.—One of the eyes in this lesson is carried out more completely, the iris and pupil being fully marked. The shades on the three different parts of the eye, though they are all subject to the same light, and afford a continuous surface, are different. Observe in the pupil the lights left between the strokes; this gives transparency.

In the ears we have an entirely different kind of line from the curves of either mouth or eyes. We have now principally lines of no definite curvature, set at various angles to one another. In the different parts of the ear two different substances are suggested by different kinds of line. In the upper part, a stiff but rather thin cartilaginous substance is designated by lines having sharp angles, themselves being rather formal and stiff; but the lobe being soft and fatty, requires rounded outlines and delicate shading. There is character to be denoted by an ear; and attention to these little details of what are often considered insignificant parts marks the true artist. From the three drawings of the ear the whole shape can be determined, and one ought to be able to draw any other position that may be required.

Lesson 34.—Here the various parts of the face are put together, at least as far as the nose, mouth, and chin are concerned, and an eye is given which may be placed by the student in its proper relative position with regard to the other features. In the profile, the projections of each lip and of the chin form a delicate curve, nearly, but not quite, a straight line. The same line carried down the full face will run through the centre of the nose, of both lips, and of the chin. Notice should be taken of the proportion of each feature, and how the slightest variation of line alters the expression.

Lesson 35.—These eyes, in various lights and positions, must be carefully studied. Not much instruction can be given as to how they are to be done beyond what has been said already, but much may be learnt from them both in the way of practice in drawing generally, and also in observation of character and expression in eyes themselves. After copying these, eyes will have a new value to the student; and if he really enters into his work, he will often find himself mentally drawing the features of those whom he sees around him: and such is excellent practice, second only to actual work upon paper, and sometimes, when combined with it, by drawing from memory the face which has been observed, it becomes one of the most valuable of an artist's acquirements. Perhaps it will be as well to notice, that the speck of light in the eye is scarcely ever so bright or so large as at first sight we are apt to imagine it.

Lesson 36.—Most of the observations made about eyes apply also to mouths, except that mouths not possessing the same brilliancy and transparency are not so much affected by the light thrown upon them; the position therefore does nct affect the appearance so much. But, on the other hand, the mouth is far more expressive than the eye, as the expressiveness is owing simply to the lines. In each of the mouths given on Plate 36 there is a slight smile, and yet how different is the expression, and that entirely without any approach to caricature or exaggeration. Compare these with a good plate of Hogarth's Laughing or Crying Audience, and the character will soon be perceptible.

Lesson 37.—The remarks on Lesson 35 will apply here also.

Lesson 38.—Noses seen at different angles will give some experience in their delineation in any position. Of more importance, however, and more difficult to imitate, is the character portrayed in the noses in the same position of profile. The first is fine and delicate, the next somewhat sharp and piquant, the third small and refined, the last heavy and coarse. Note the slight distinctions that make these differences of idea, and another step will have been made towards conveying character in a face.

Lesson 39.—We now come to the limbs; and before beginning to copy this foot, it will be perhaps as well to look back and compare it with some of the leaves or the flasks that have been given before. In them the curves were regular and the opposite sides corresponded, but here no two parts are alike. It is more than ever necessary now to attend to the general outline first, leaving the smaller details, such as the division of the toes and the slight re-entering curves, until the main form is well determined. Mark, too, the depth of tone on the lower side of each part, and the slight shade which indicates the cavity beneath the instep.

Lesson 40.—A delicacy of treatment and an accuracy of outline in the hands of a figure are distinguishing marks of a great painter. Especial care, therefore, should be bestowed upon the next four lessons. In the first, whilst the whole hand is indicated, the portion which is especially brought under notice is the thumb; whereas in the next

(Lesson 41), the hand being in the same position, but seen from a different point of view, gives the fingers principally, and hints only at the thumb. The two copies should be carefully compared together, so that the different characters of the parts may be remarked; and the strength and decision of the thumb contrasted with the delicacy and roundness of the fingers. Note, too, the slight variety of the lines which indicate the back of the hand. In both cases the roll grasped will assist in keeping the various parts in proportion, and will form starting-points from which the more complicated outlines may begin. In the lower line of the thumb, each of the projections indicates a muscle, which changes in elevation with every motion of the hand. The shading, be it noted, follows the curves of the flesh, whilst the deep shadow of the roll softens off and gives a round-ness to the hand.

Lesson 41.—The lines between the fingers are dark, because they serve as outlines on both sides, and assist the shading in rounding the fingers, be-tween which they lie. One general line for the lower part of the thumb and the three latter fingers will assist in keeping these in their places. It will be well to observe that these outlines are more angular, and approach more closely to straight lines. The slight shades are all-important: they mark out the projections of knuckles and muscles. Let the bones of the wrist be clearly demonstrated.

Lesson 42.—Both thumb and fingers are here combined, so that their relative value may be more clearly seen and copied. Notice the muscularity and boniness of the former compared with the fleshy roundness of the latter. In the thumb, as here seen, the joints are scarcely indicated, except by the curve in the outline, and so too in the last joints of the fingers. Great care therefore must be taken that these curves correspond on the opposite sides of the member.

Lesson 43.—As before thumbs were compared with fingers, so in this lesson the female arm is compared with the male, and the female hand with the male. The difference here observable is to be found in many other parts besides the arm. In the one case we get delicate lines, flowing curves, general roundness; in the other we see firmer lines, shorter and more abrupt curves, muscles developed so as to break the delicate roundness, and to give strength and solidity to the limb. The number of strokes in the male is far greater than in the female; but it will be found that it is more difficult to give the effect of the few delicate strokes than of the numerous hard and characteristic lines. Each of the indentations represents the termination of a muscle, and requires therefore as much accuracy as any portion of the outlines. In all the hands in this plate the muscles not being in action are but slightly developed, consequently we have more roundness, both in the hands themselves and in the wrists and arms, than we should have if violent action were going on in the fingers or hands. Observe how delicately the nails are delineated. One very common mistake with beginners is to make these very noticeable but gently indicated marks, and the similar markings in lips, &c., a great deal too dark or too prominent. The slightest hint at their position is quite enough to suggest them to the mind which is already prepared to see that which it knows to be there.

Lesson 44.—Again we have the contrast between the extremities of the female and male figure. The same differences are observable here as in the upper limbs. The deep dark shade and the strong development of muscle again mark the masculine character. The toes, too, exhibit a diversity amongst themselves. Notice the division between the great toe and the others, not so great of course as between the thumb and fingers, but still far more distinctly marked than between any of the other toes. The slight shadings on the male foot show where the numerous bones come. Beneath each foot there is a certain amount of shadow—without this the limbs would be suspended in air. One of the main difficulties in drawing feet, and the difficulties are scarcely less than in drawing hands, consists in making them stand firmly upon the ground. Next to accuracy of outline, the shadow beside the foot contributes most to this end.

Lesson 45.—The foot here is in motion, only slightly touching the ground, and consequently only having a shadow at the toe. Great care will be required to draw this accurately, because as the heel retires it will be foreshortened, and the slightest inaccuracy will cause the appearance of a great swelling, or of a wondrous deficiency. Notice how the great toe, being the one most bent, and consequently that lies flattest on the ground and retires most abruptly, narrows towards the base. The shade down the side of the foot marks the projection of a strong muscle and gives the shape of this portion of the foot. Given too darkly it would cause the idea of a bulging protuberance ; but if it is not dark enough, or is put out of place, it will produce an appearance of deformity and ugliness. The direction of the lines upwards by the ankle suggests the shape of the leg above, and a slight change of angle will make all the difference between a thick stumpy limb, and a thin spare bone.

Lesson 46.—In this lesson, and in the succeeding one, we have the whole of the features combined. After having practised each individually with some attention, it will be found possible to connect them, and to produce them in proportion. Of course considerable care will now be required, but principally in these matters of proportionate size, and fitting relationship the one to the other. A delicate curve may be made the starting line from which the features spring. This can be divided so as to mark off the parts, fixing the place of eye, nose, and mouth. Then the features can be drawn as easily as they have been in the previous larger copies. After this the shape of the head should engage the attention, then the position of the ear, and, lastly, the rest of the figure. The hair, which at first looks difficult, will be found easy enough if the copy is studied sufficiently. The strokes, which of course are curved, come to something like a point. It will probably be found that the mouth and eye present most difficulty, because the slightest variation in a single stroke alters the entire expression.

Lesson 47.—The remarks on Lesson 46 will apply equally well to this copy. The rounding is less than in the former plate, so that the shade on the face is even lighter in this instance.

Lesson 48.—This will no doubt be attractive enough to many of our readers, but it will require all its attractiveness to make the drawing of it satisfactory; for there is far more difficulty than the ardent young student will see at first. Here we have motion; every muscle is excited; even that straight tail, which will wag the moment we say a word. A straight line from the ear to the middle of the fore paw, the same length as from the latter to the root of the tail, gives a general idea of the direction of the various lines. Again, a line in the direction of the tail crosses the lowest hollow of the back, and cuts the shoulder at the junction of the collar. Many such measurements as these the student may find for himself. The shading should be minutely copied; for, as the learner will have found by this time, each line has its value, the direction and size of the lines generally giving the character of the short stiff hair of the dog, whilst the direction of the shading gives the line of muscle or of bone. Notice, too, the value of each stroke towards suggesting the character of rough herbage upon which lies distinctly the shadow which throws forward the dog.

Lesson 49.—The dog's head is of a very different character from the figure of a dog in the last lesson. Not only is the breed not the same—the former was a pointer, and here we have a mastiff—but the idea to be impressed on the mind is essentially altered. Here we have rest combined with massive power; before we had action and excitement. This is to be seen in the character of line used. Before we had rounded soft and short lines; here we have square and solid strokes. Note this squareness throughout. One can almost take hold of the fleshy jowl. This reality is due to the short, sharp, firm lines which form its outline. Further variety of practice is afforded by the eye and nose in the corners.

Lesson 50.—A whole figure, that of a French fisher-girl, concludes the present series. As in the case of the features combined into whole heads, so here, where all the limbs are combined into the entire figure, the principal difficulty will be found to consist in the proper proportions. Each limb should be realized beneath the clothing, which hangs from the projecting points. Notice how all the lower lines are deeper than the upper ones of the same surface. The hanging of the net is indicated by the lines of the folds. The distant line of the sea is perfectly level and horizontal. The shadows from the feet and boards cause the figure to stand firmly on the ground.

Concluding Remarks.—It will have been seen in the above examples how a gradual advance may be made by taking the simplest forms at first, by adding them together, and by taking care to keep the right proportions between them. Care, attention, cleanliness, and accuracy, all contribute to the power of correctly copying any work that it may be required to reproduce. But, besides these, there is requisite a great deal of experience to be gained only by imitating good works of great artists, and by a careful study of nature itself. People talk about genius being the chief requisite to make a good draughtsman. The principal genius to be desired in this matter, as in most others, is such a delight in works of art as leads to constant and continuous practice, such an appreciation of one's own works as will induce us to go on in spite of frequent and serious failures, and such a sense of one's own mistakes as will cause a vigorous endeavour to amend in future performances.

PLATES.

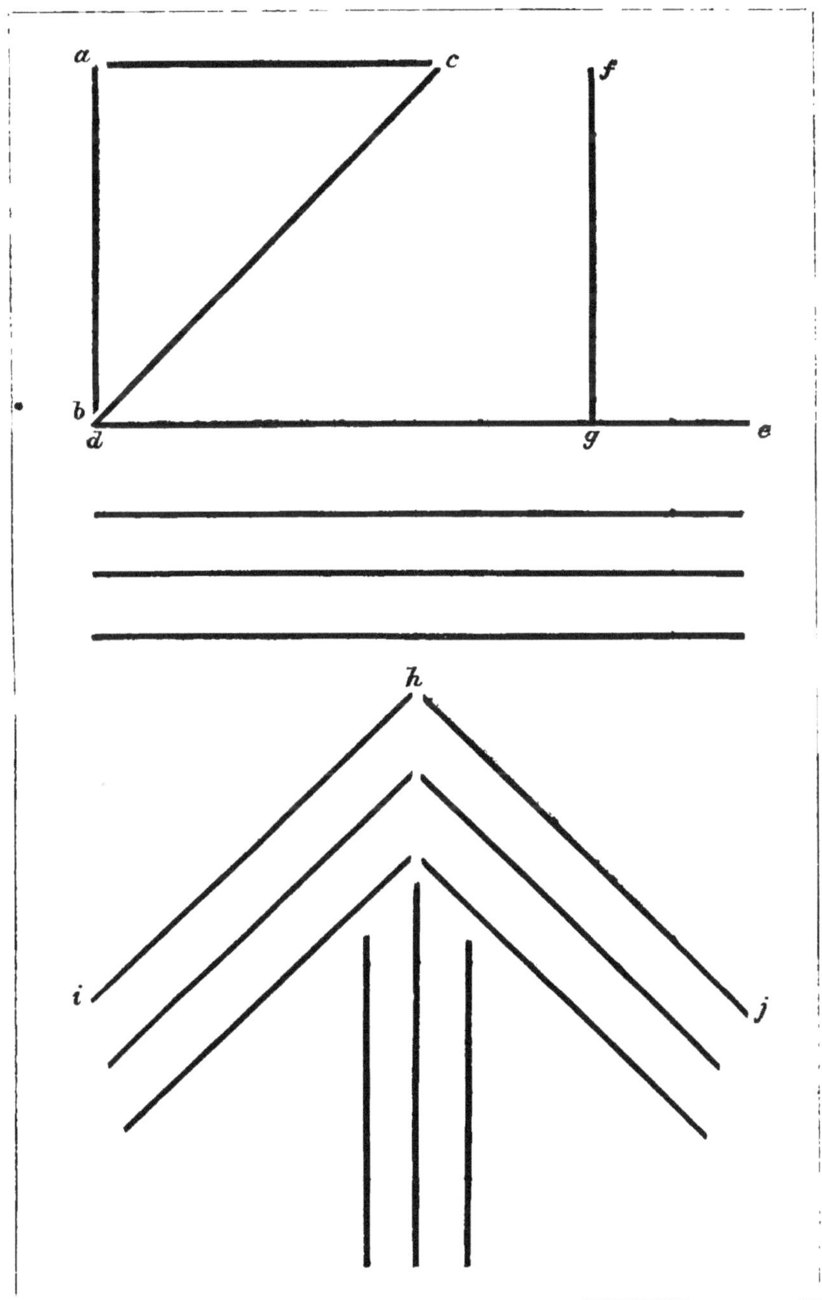

a
c
f
b
d
g
e
h
i
j

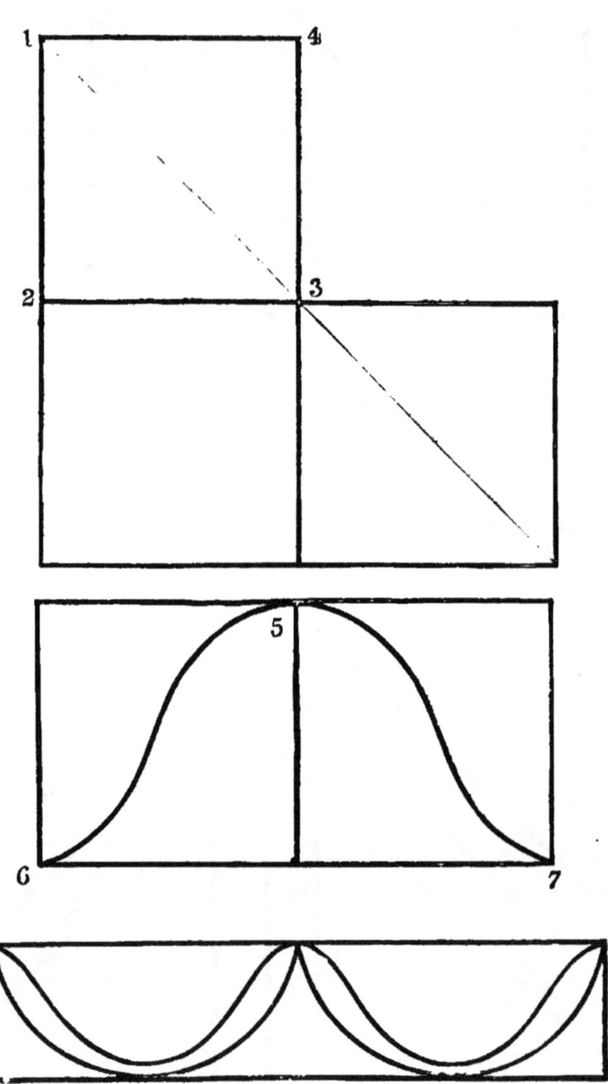

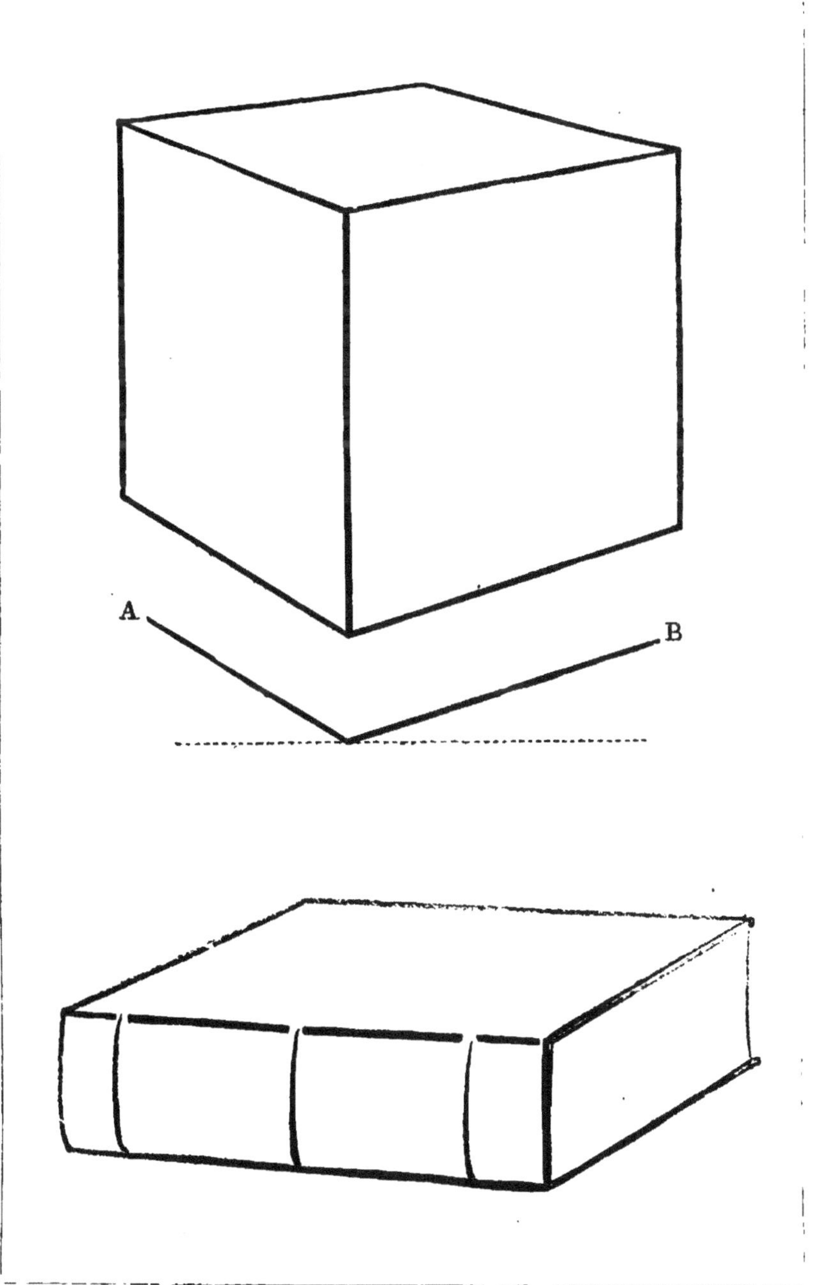
A
B

A
B
C
D

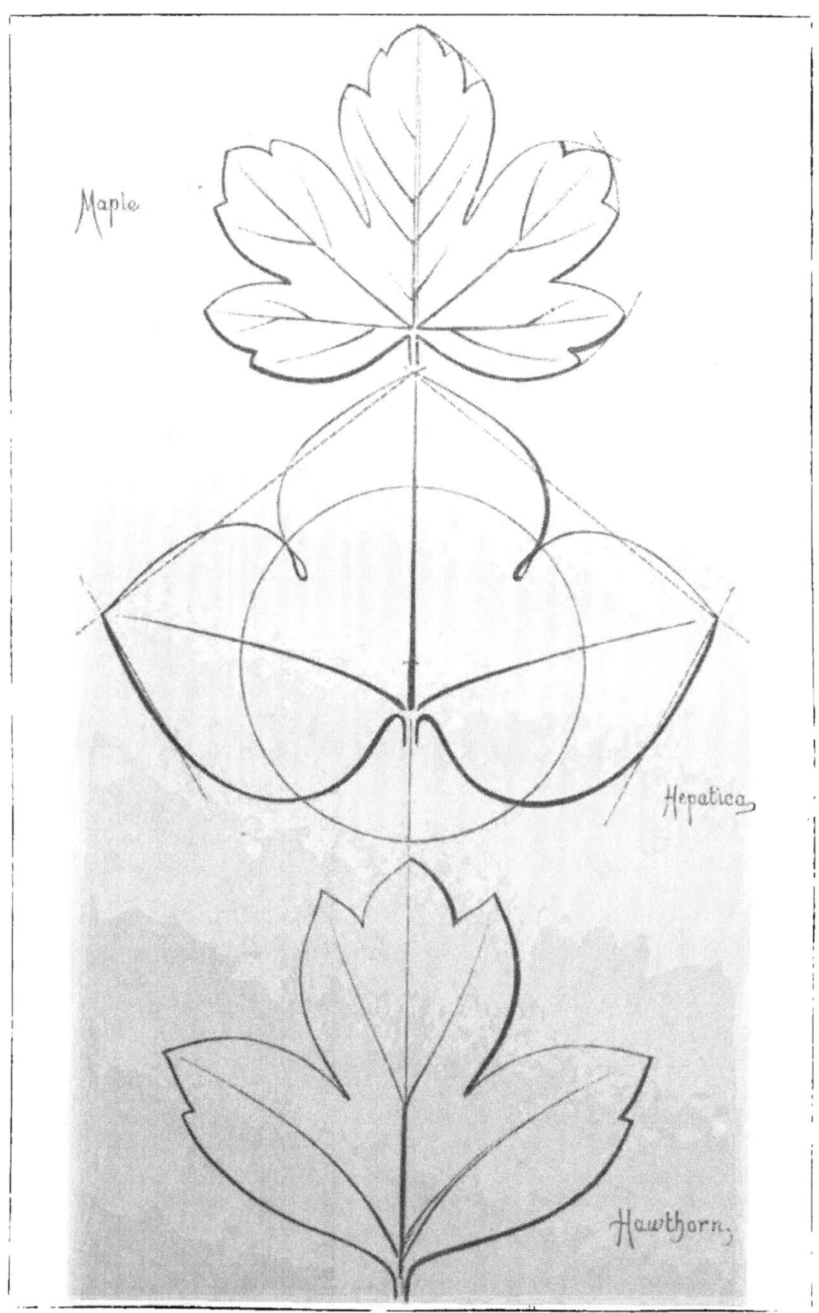
Maple
Hepatica
Hawthorn

Ivy
Golden Saxifrage
Meadow Saxifrage
Passion flower

Oak
Ground Ivy
Spinach

Lesson 8.

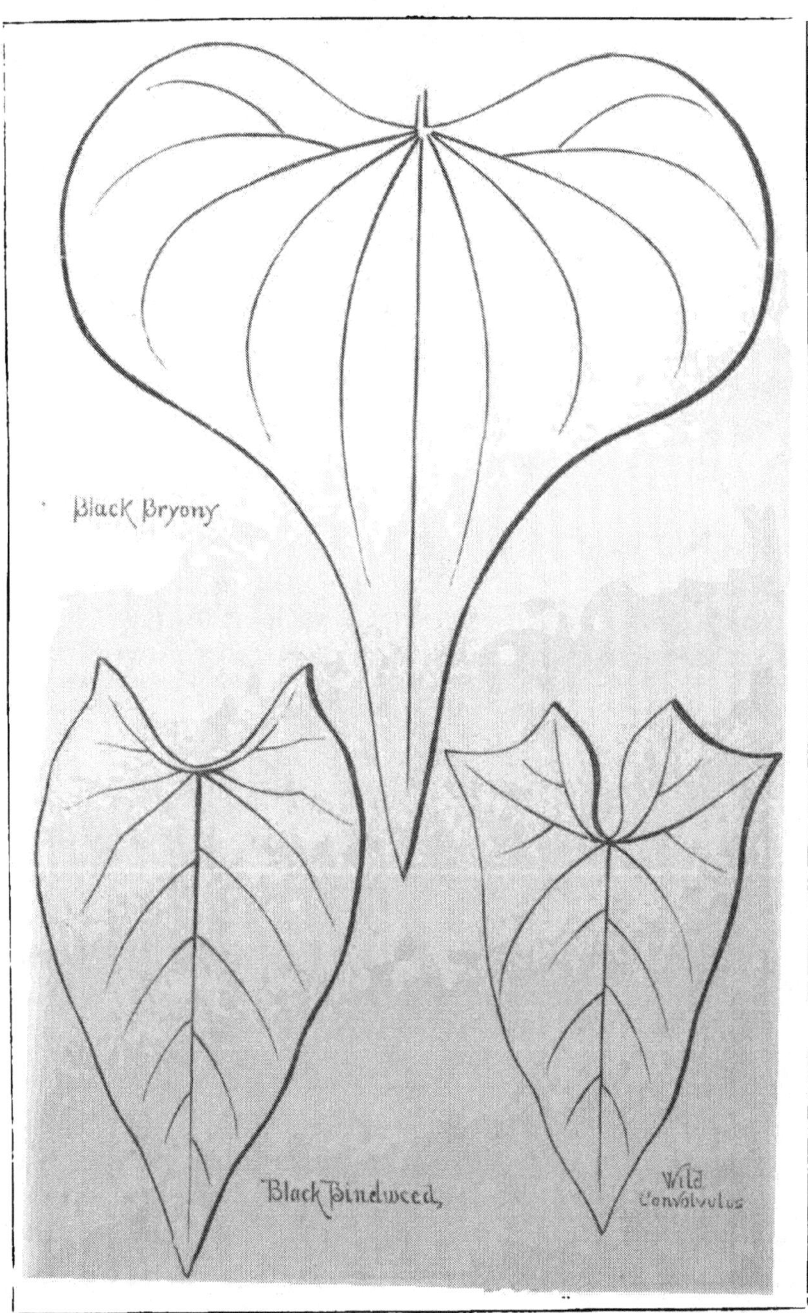

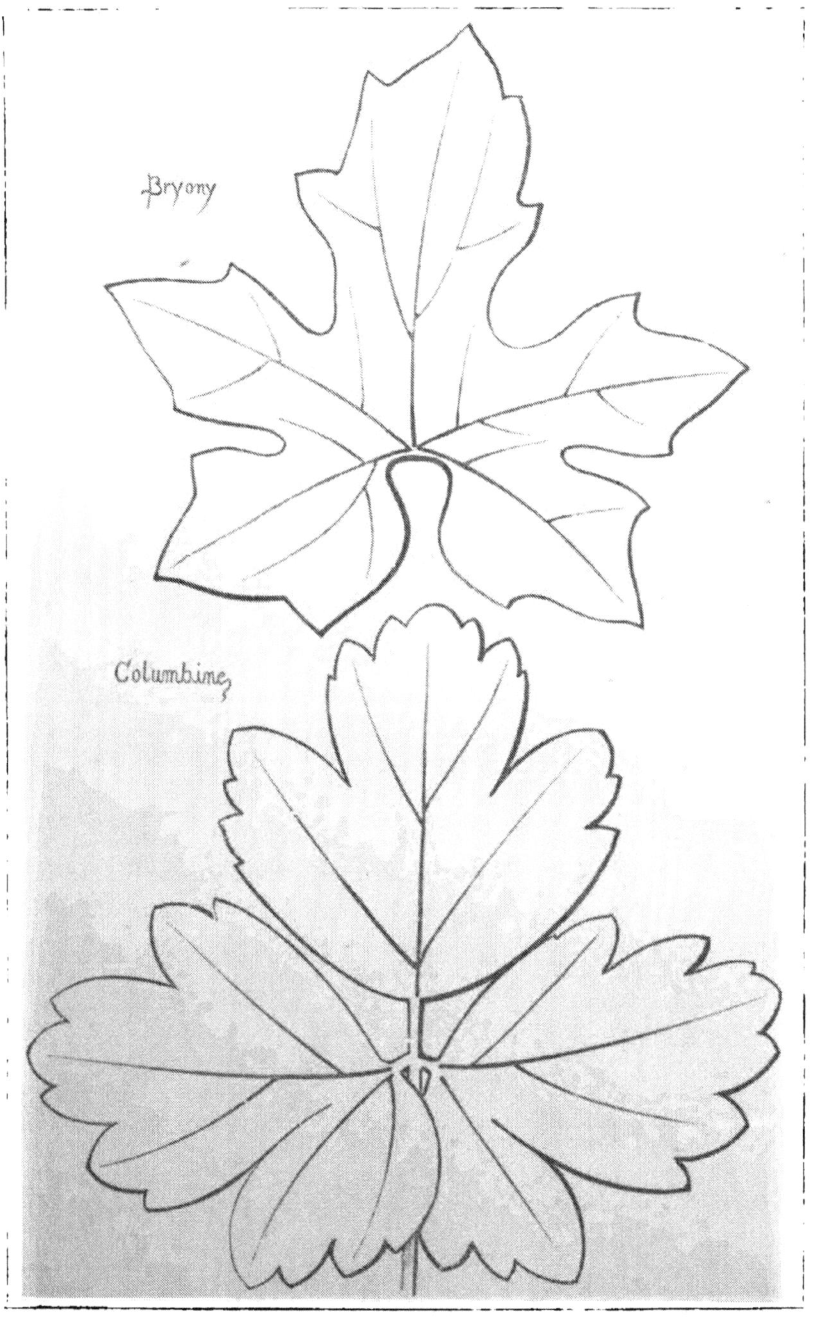
Bryony
Columbine

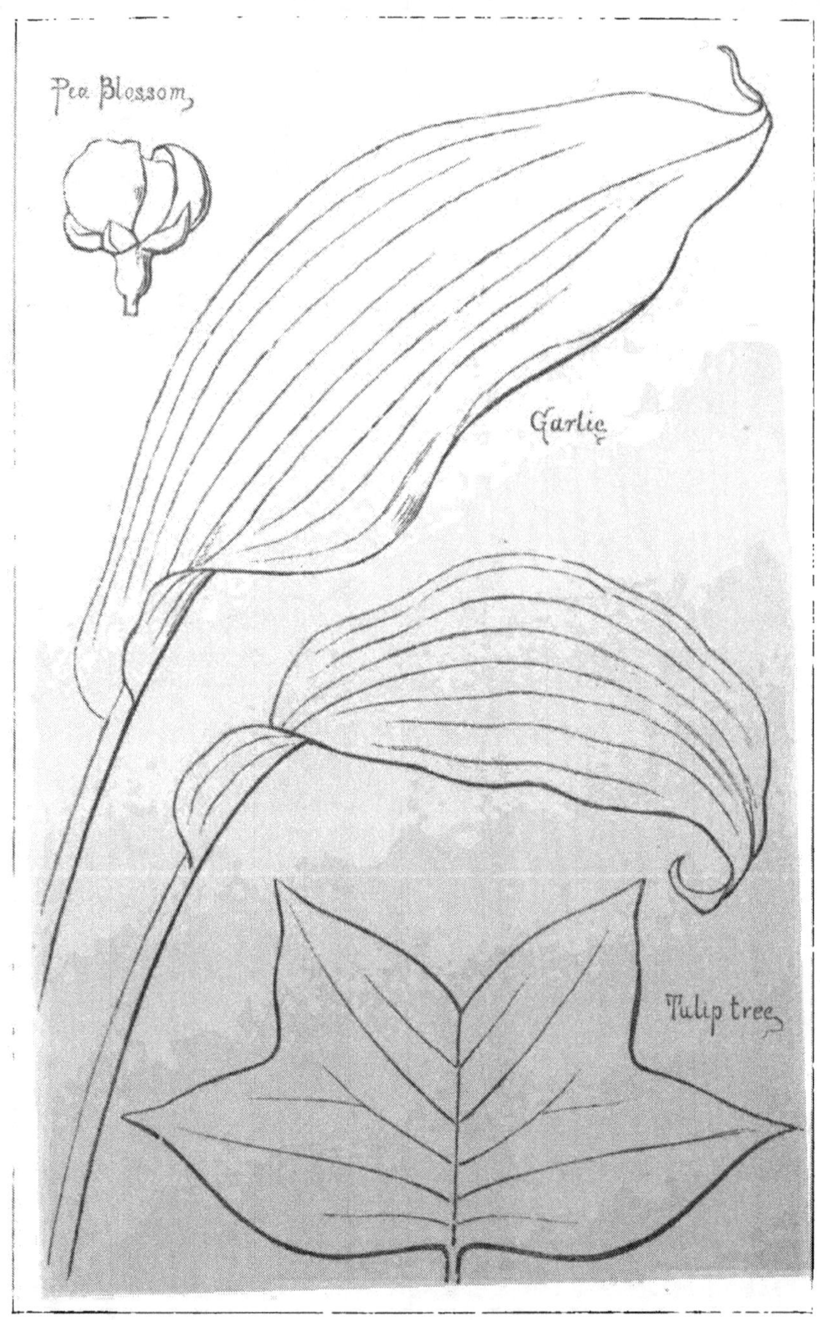
Pea Blossom,
Garlic
Tulip tree

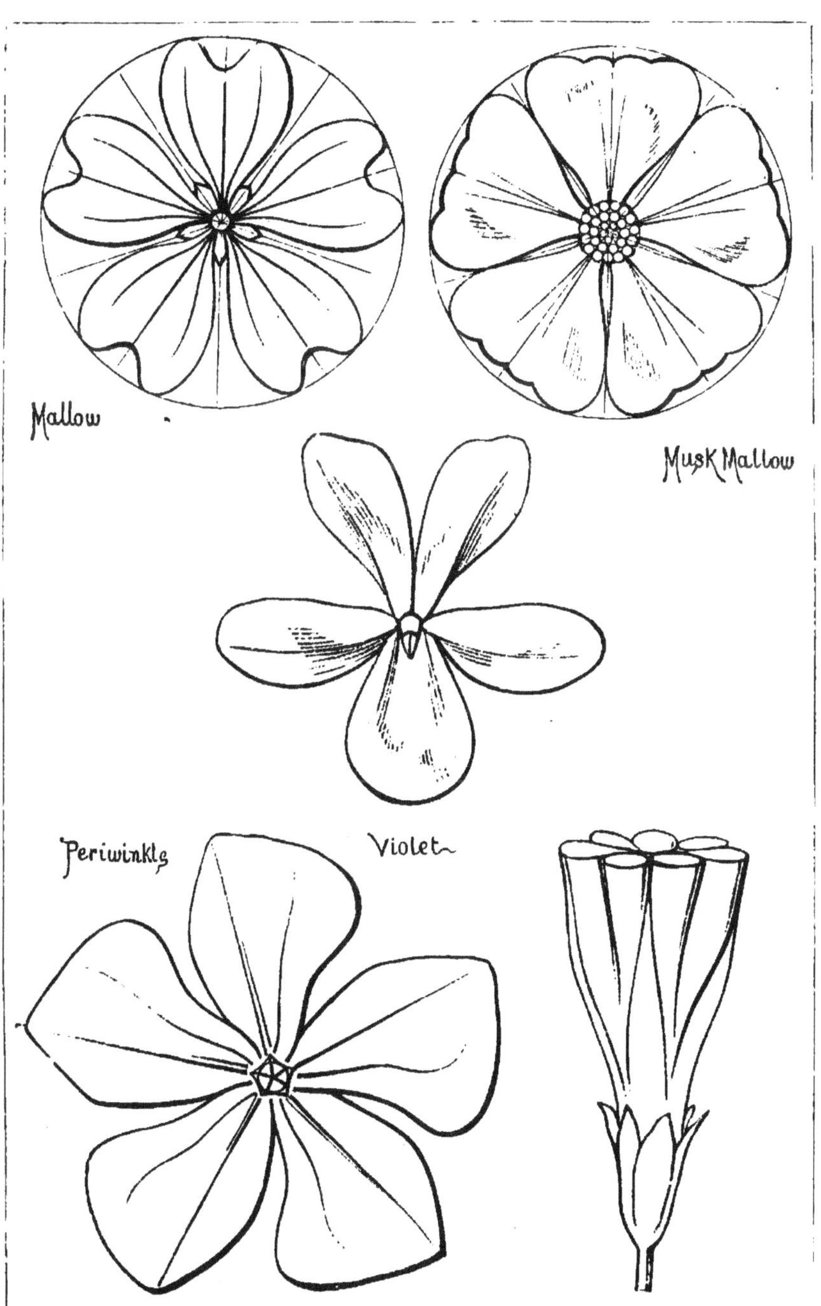
Mallow
Musk Mallow
Periwinkle
Violet

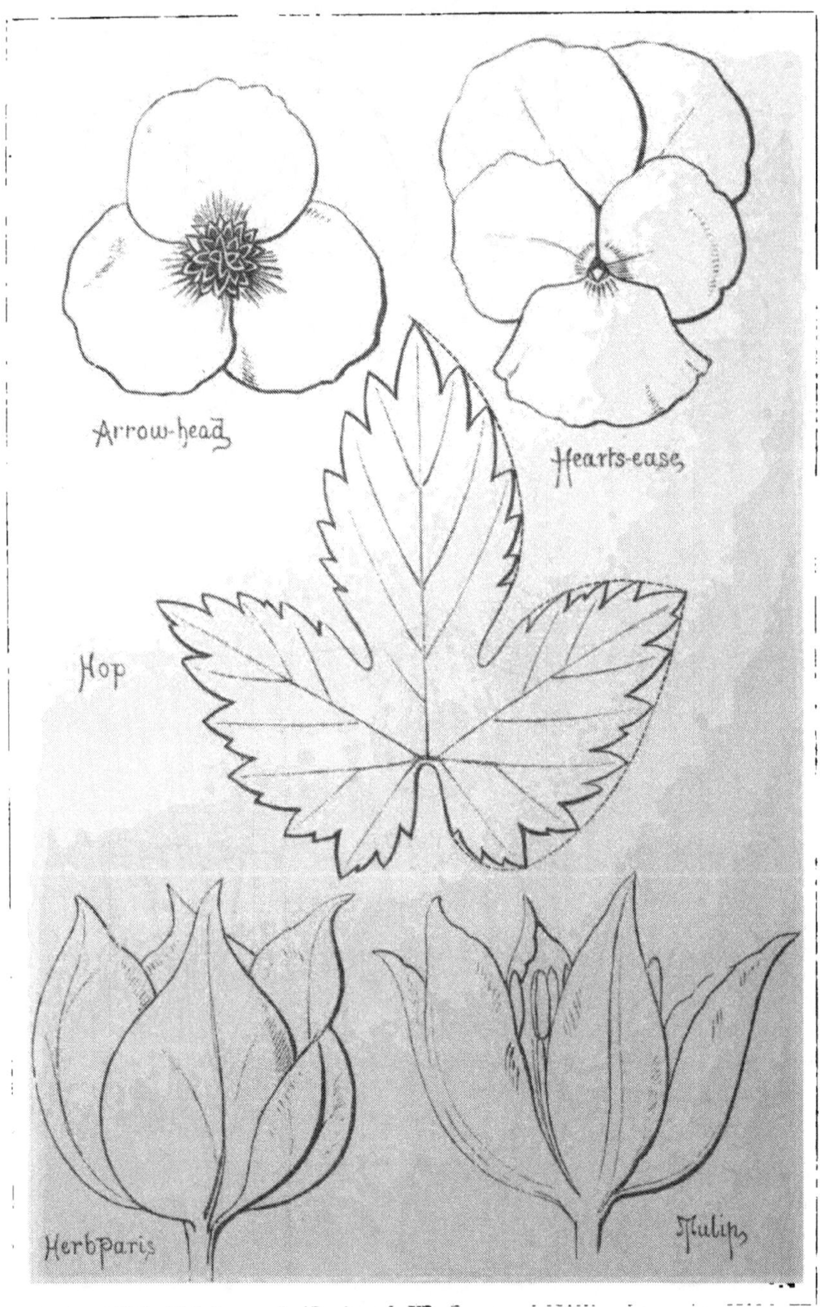
Arrow-head
Hearts-ease
Hop
Herb Paris
Tulip

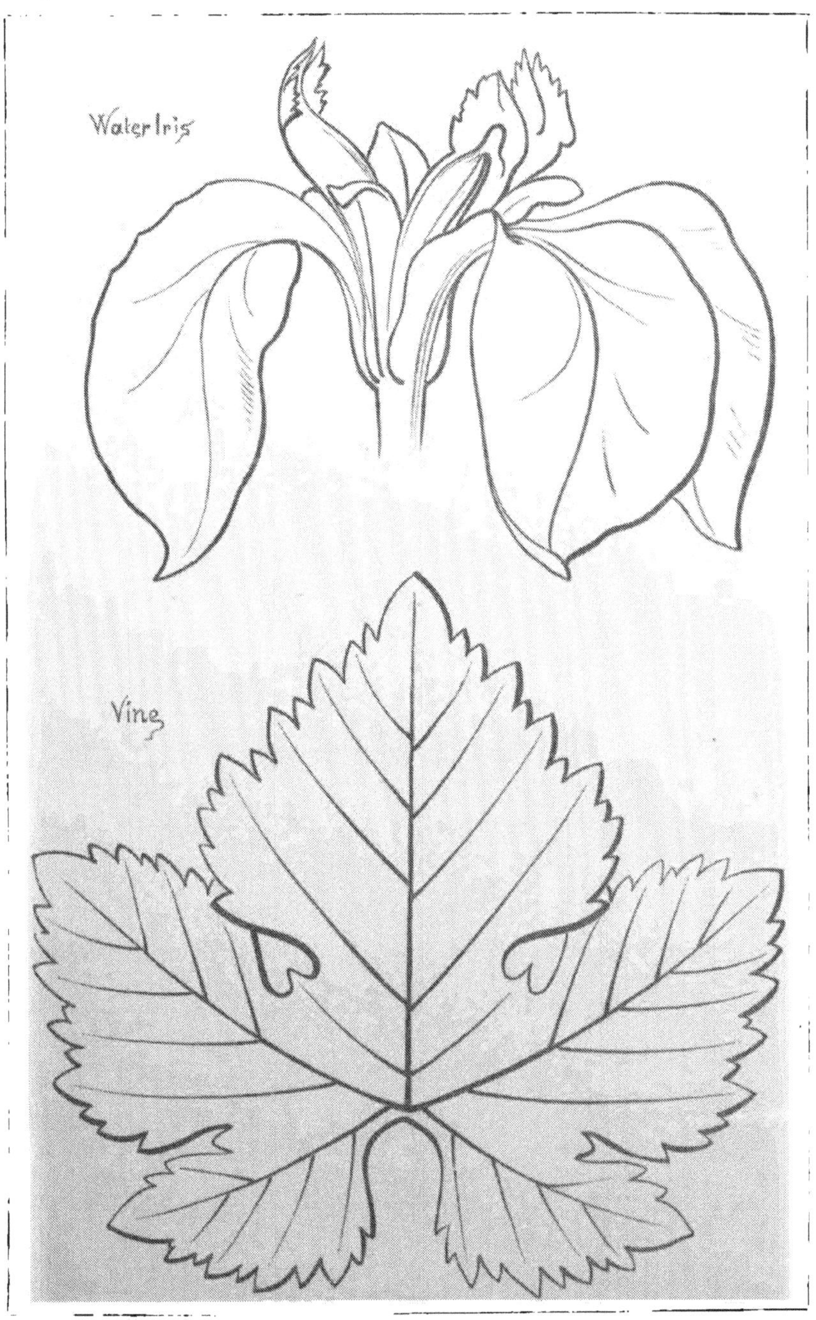
Water Iris
Vine

Holly

Horned Poppy
Autumn
Crocus

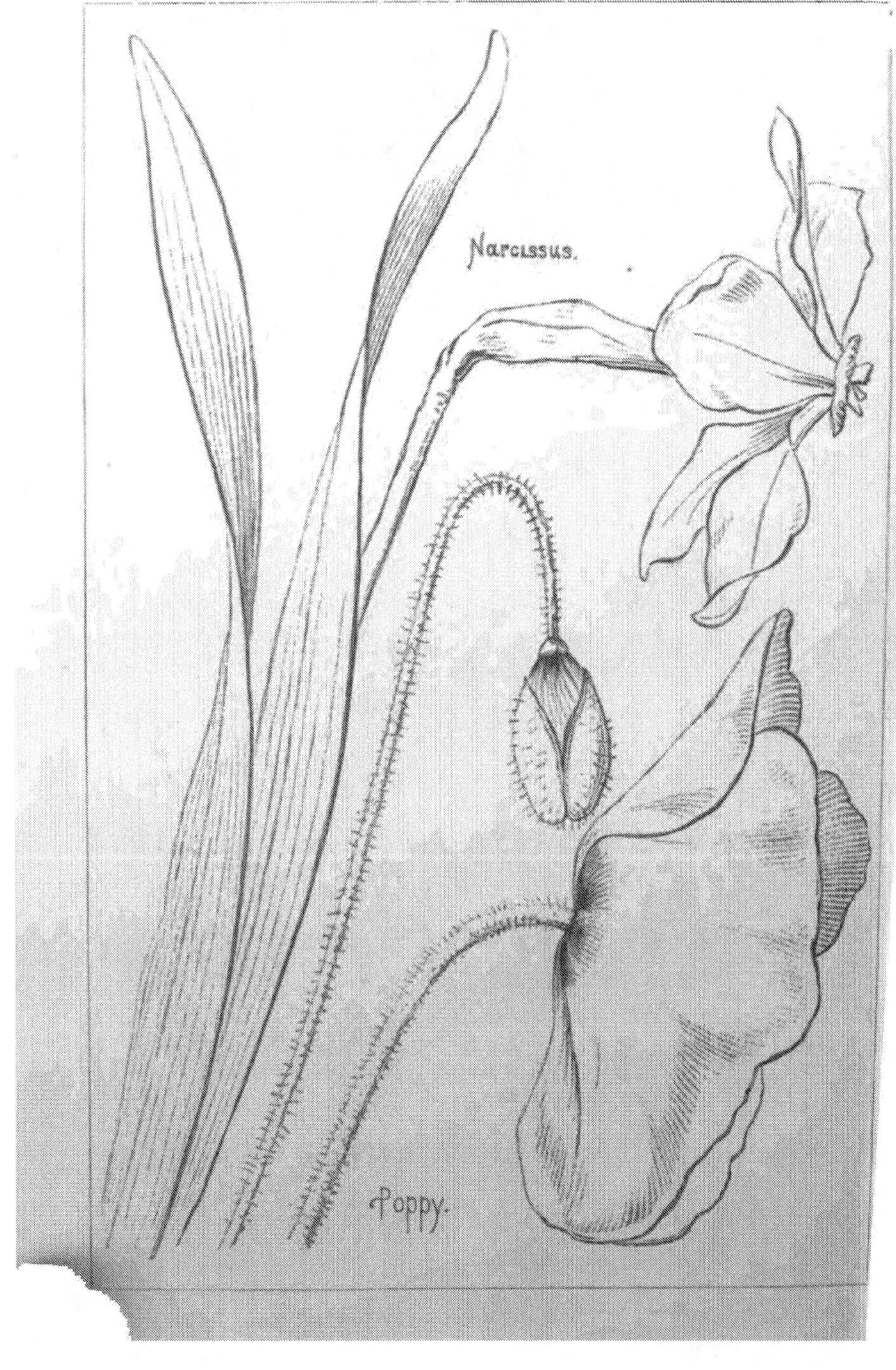
Narcissus.
Poppy.

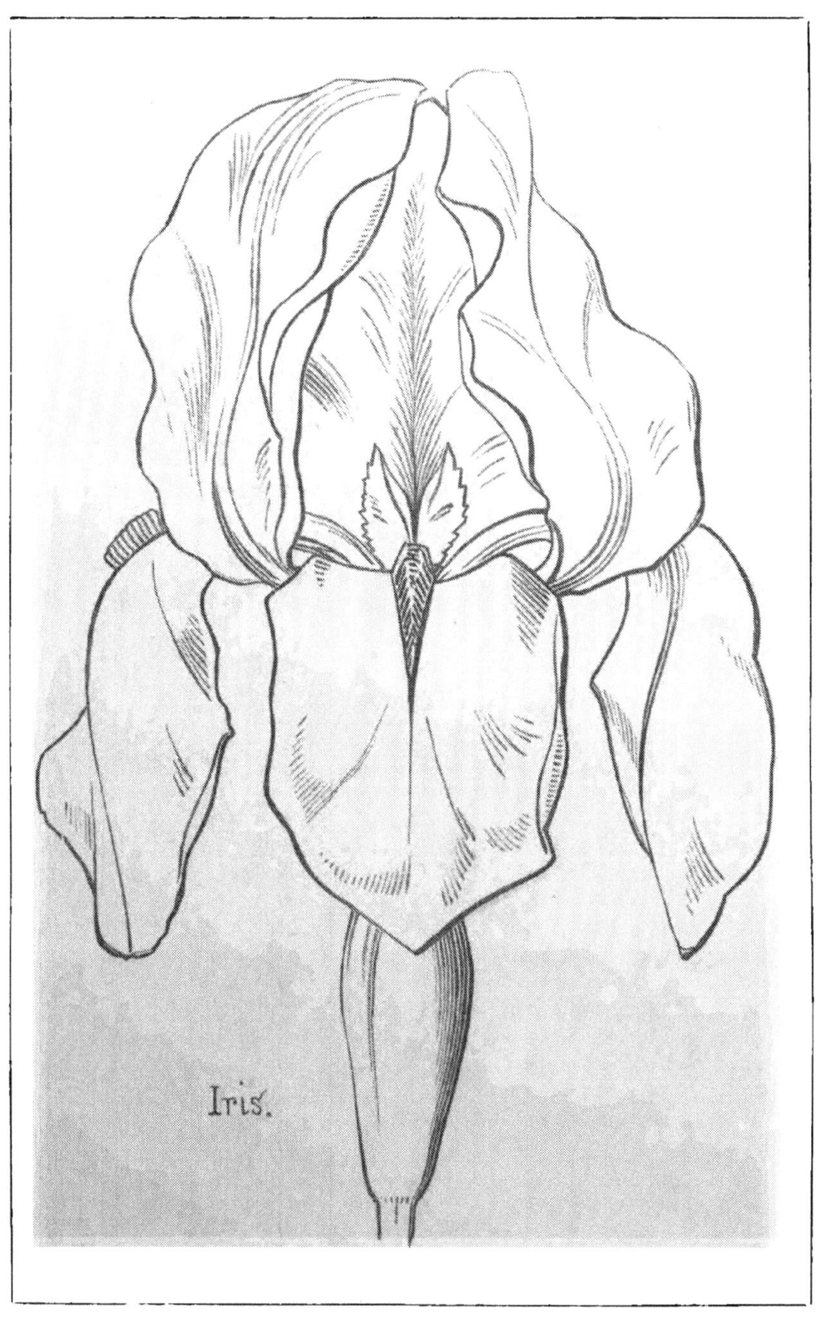
Iris.

Petunia

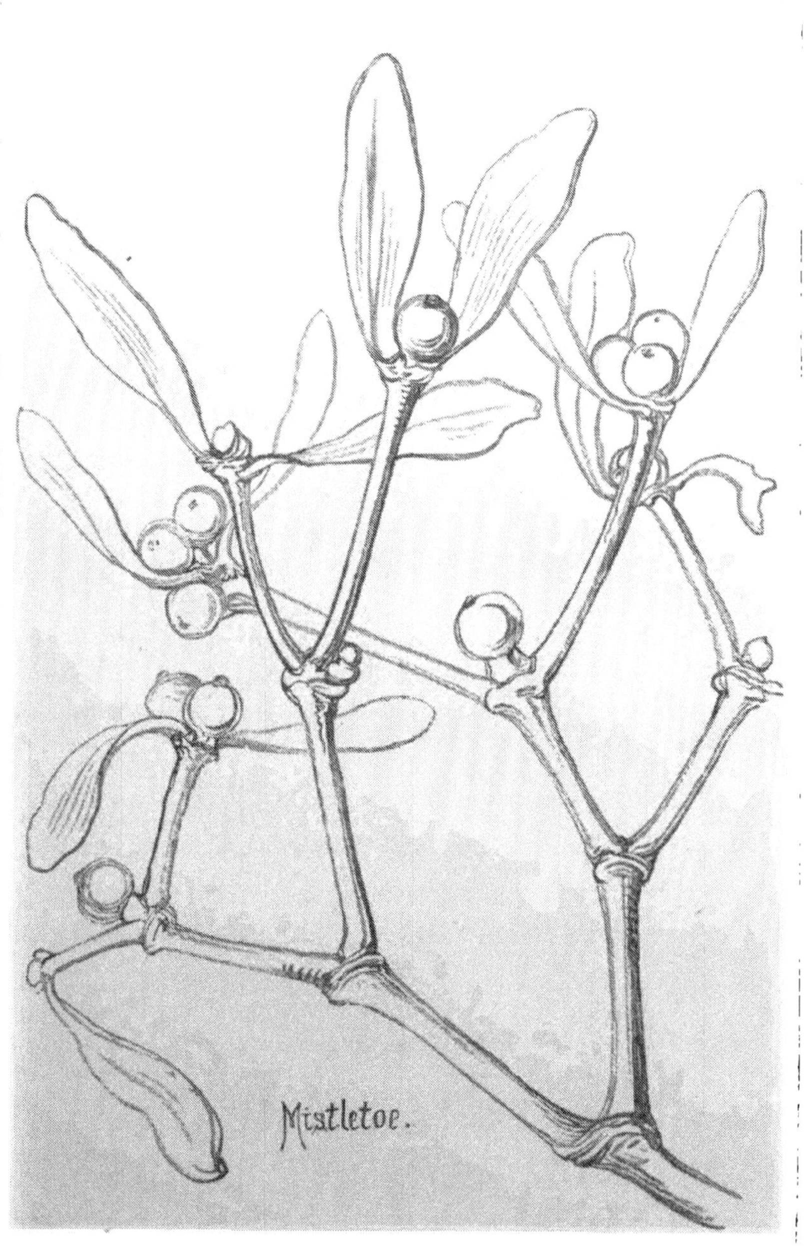

Mistletoe.

Narcissus.

Snapdragon

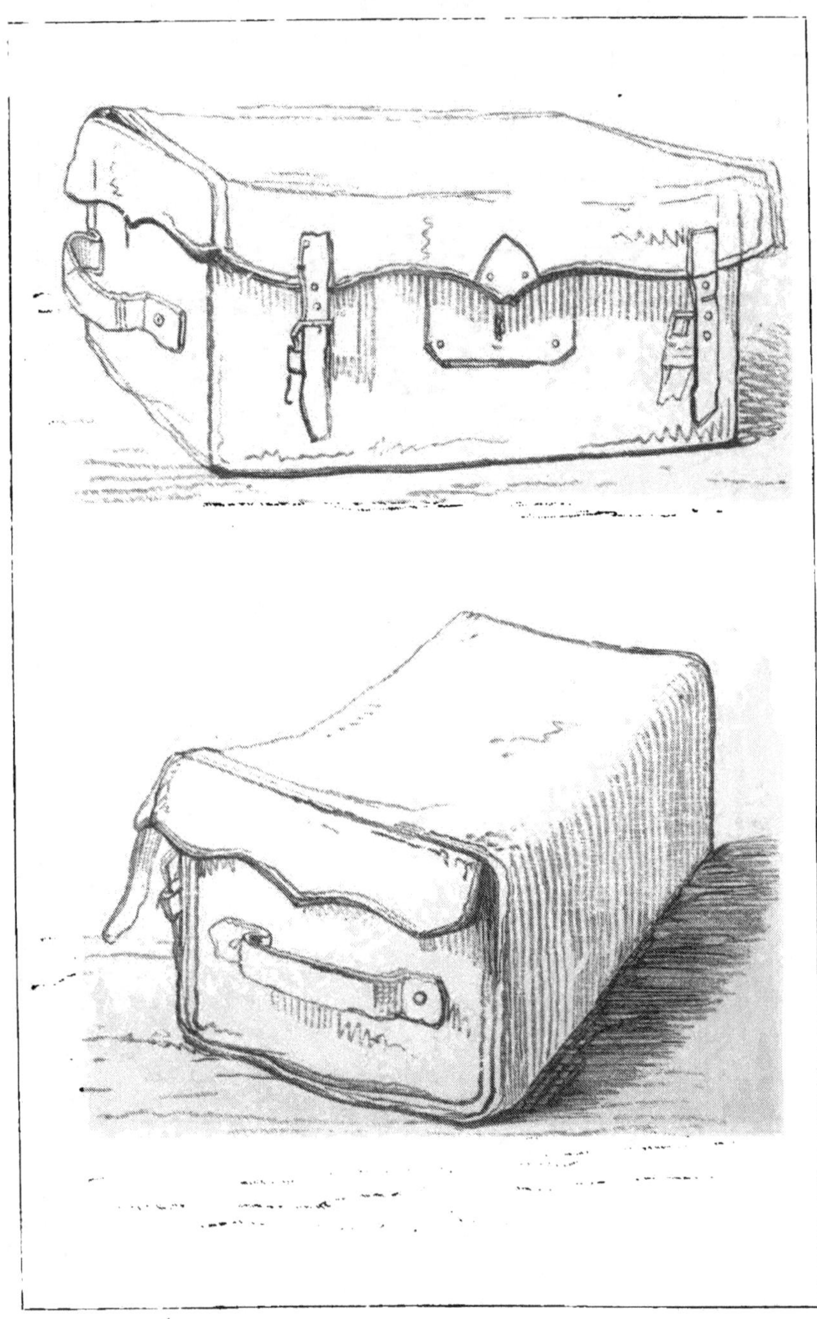

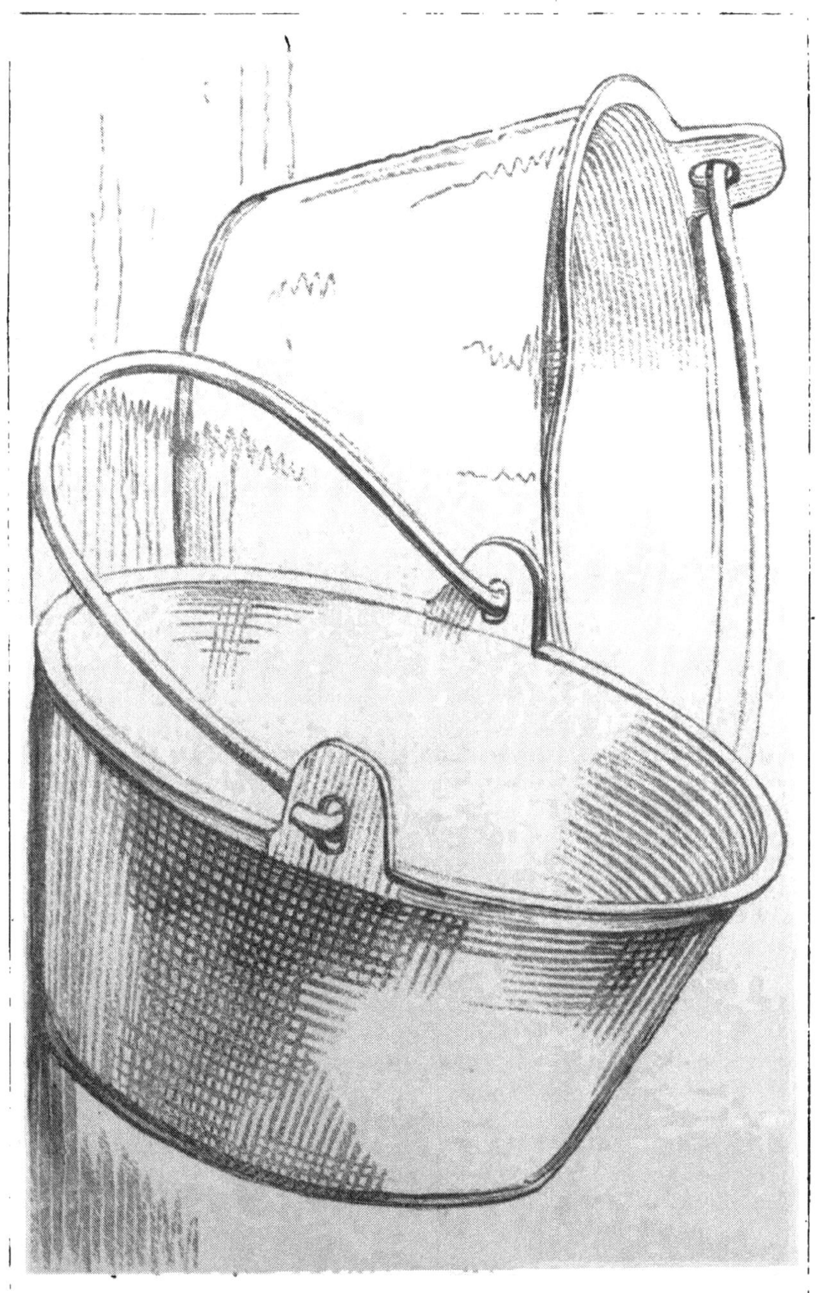

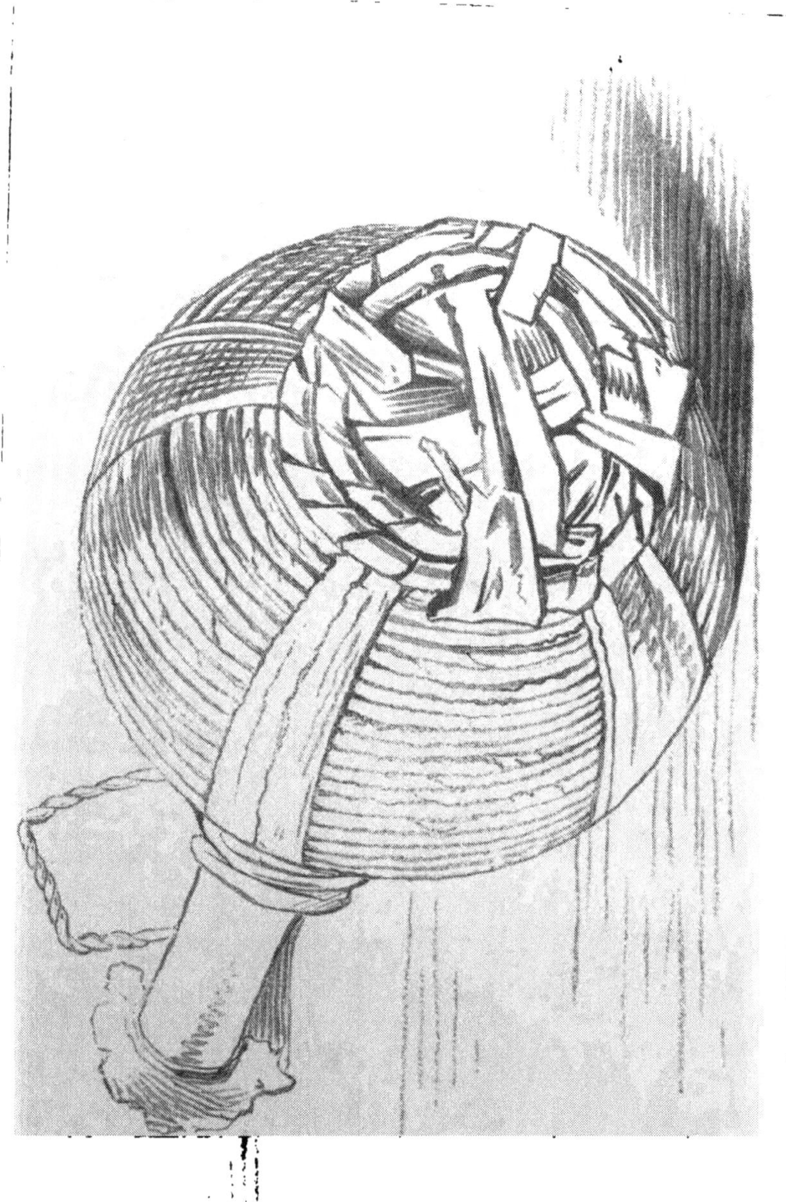

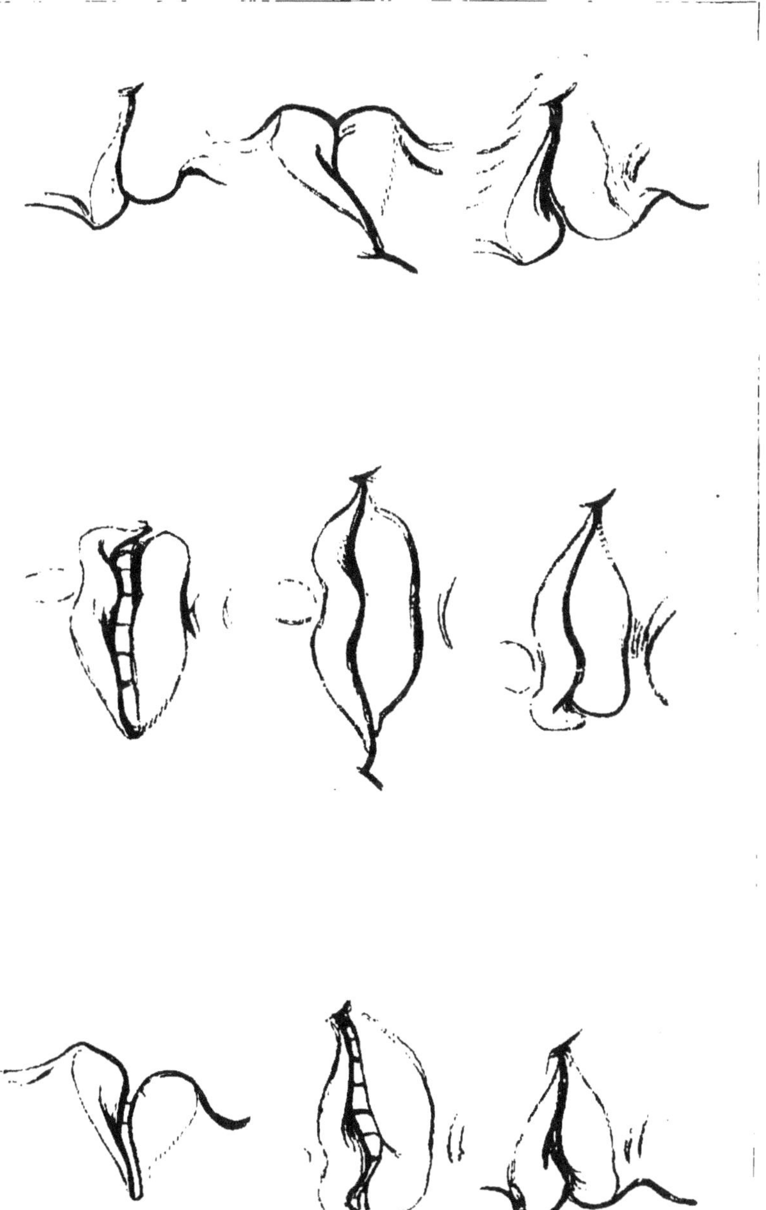

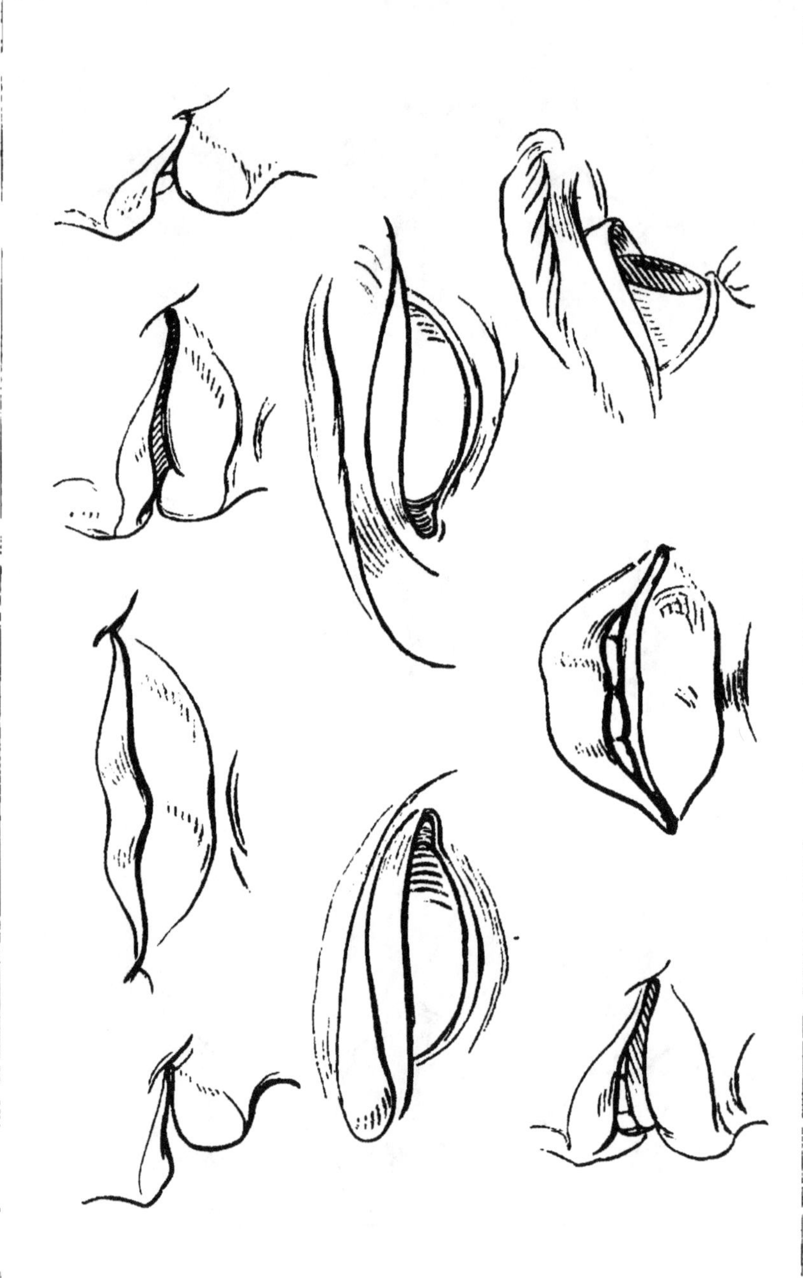

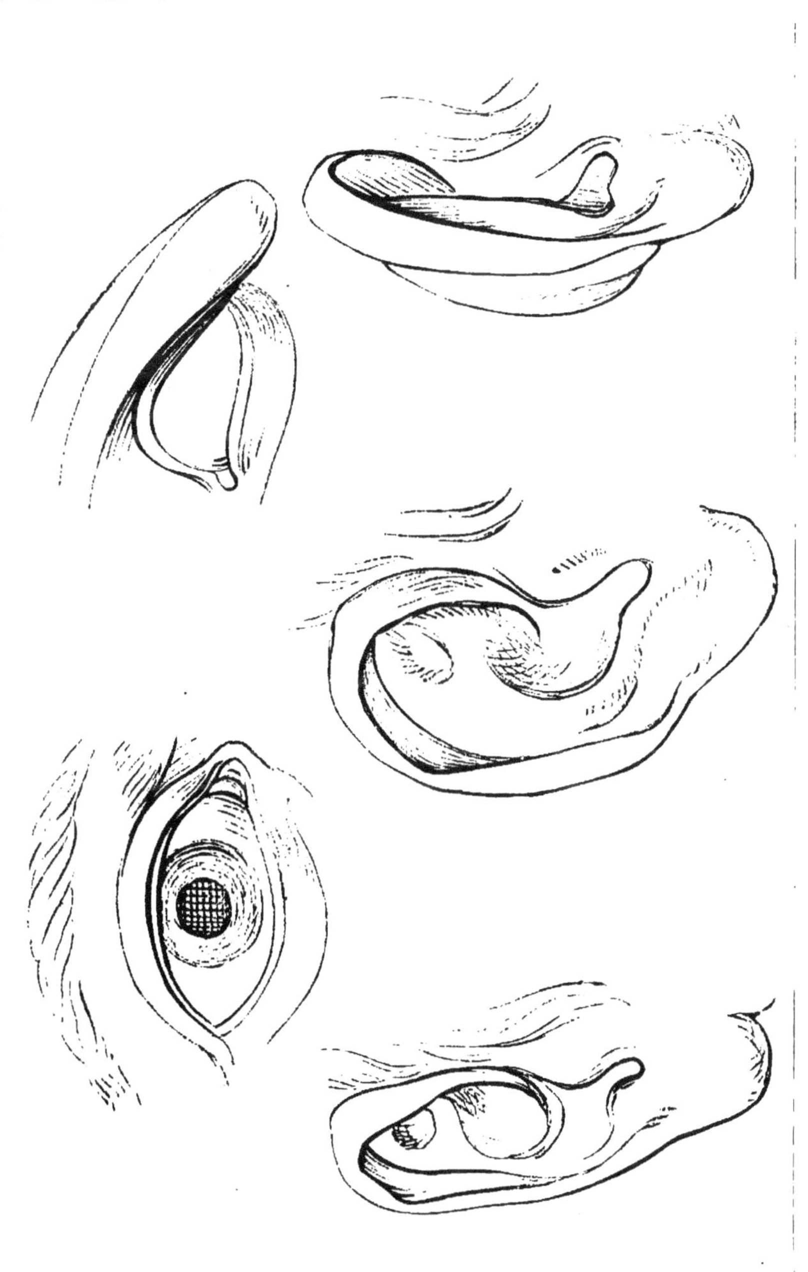

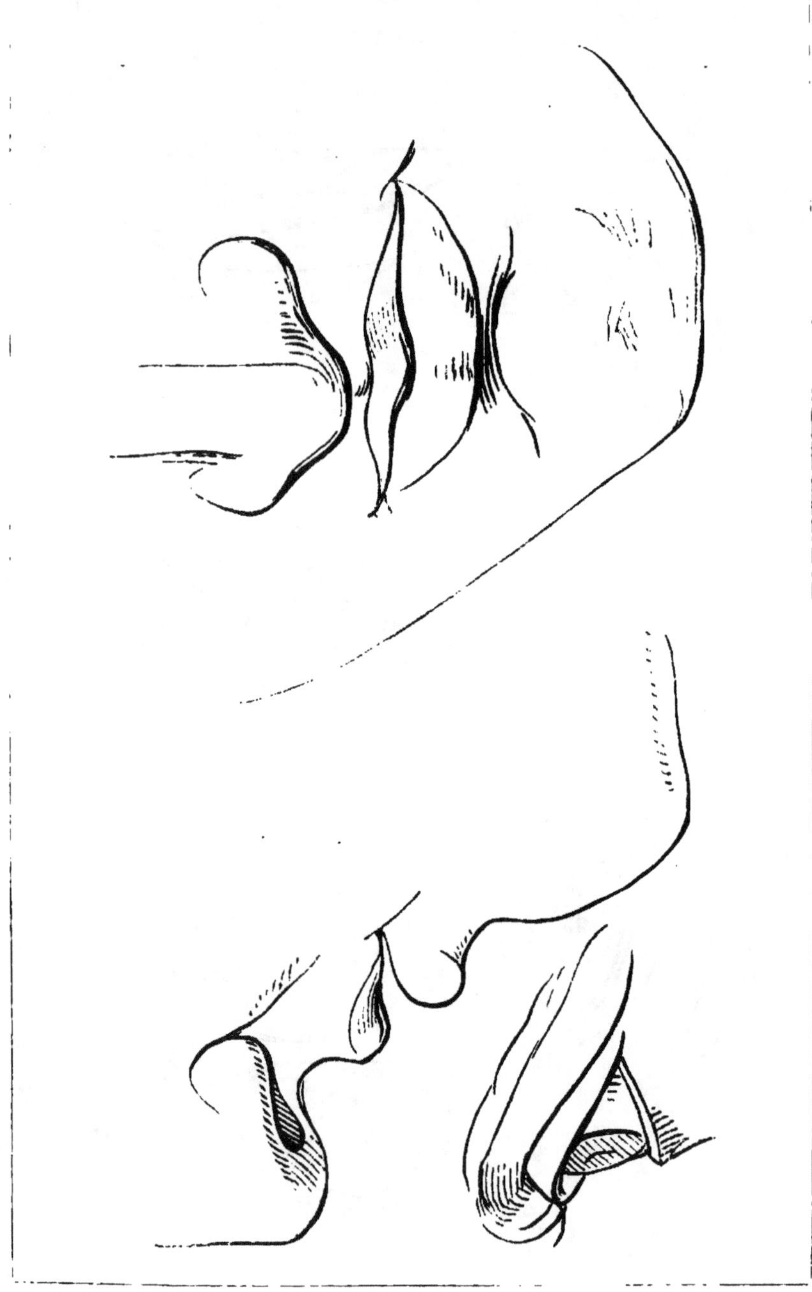

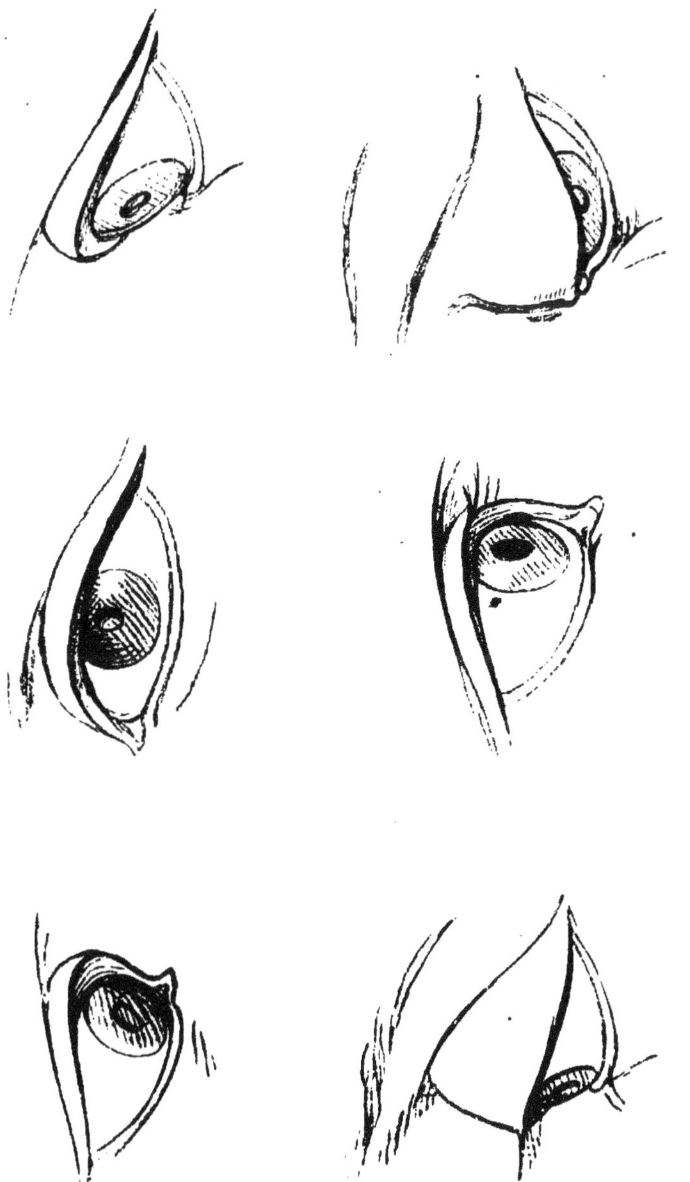

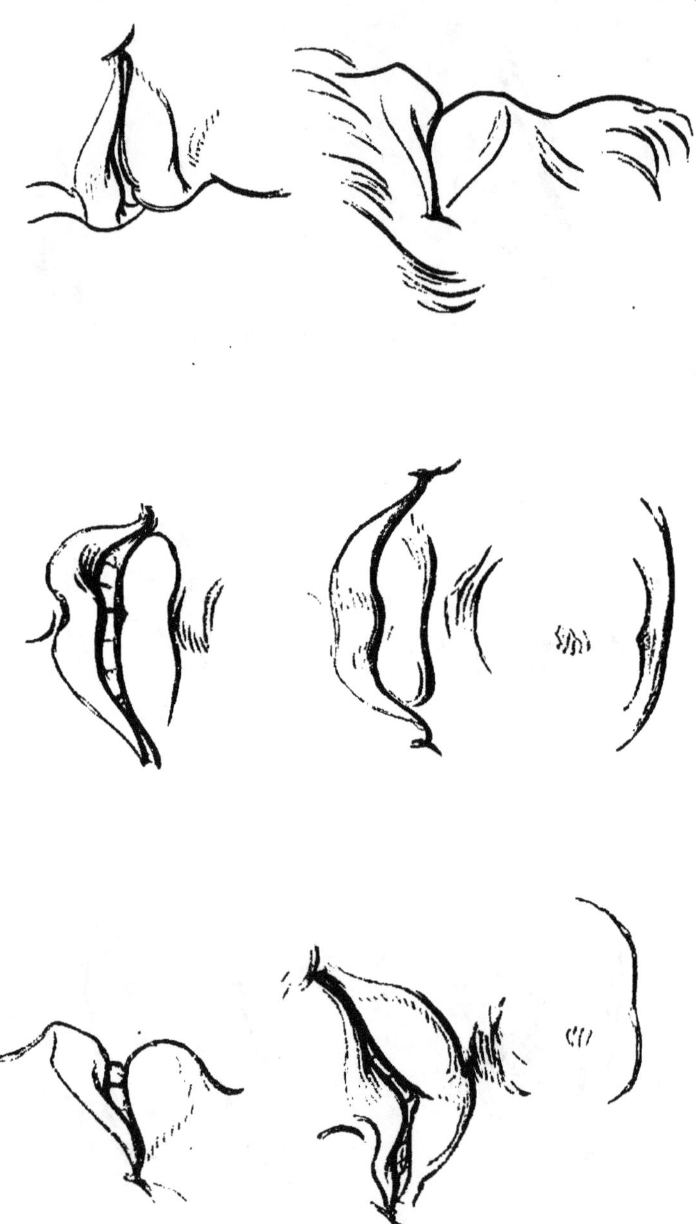

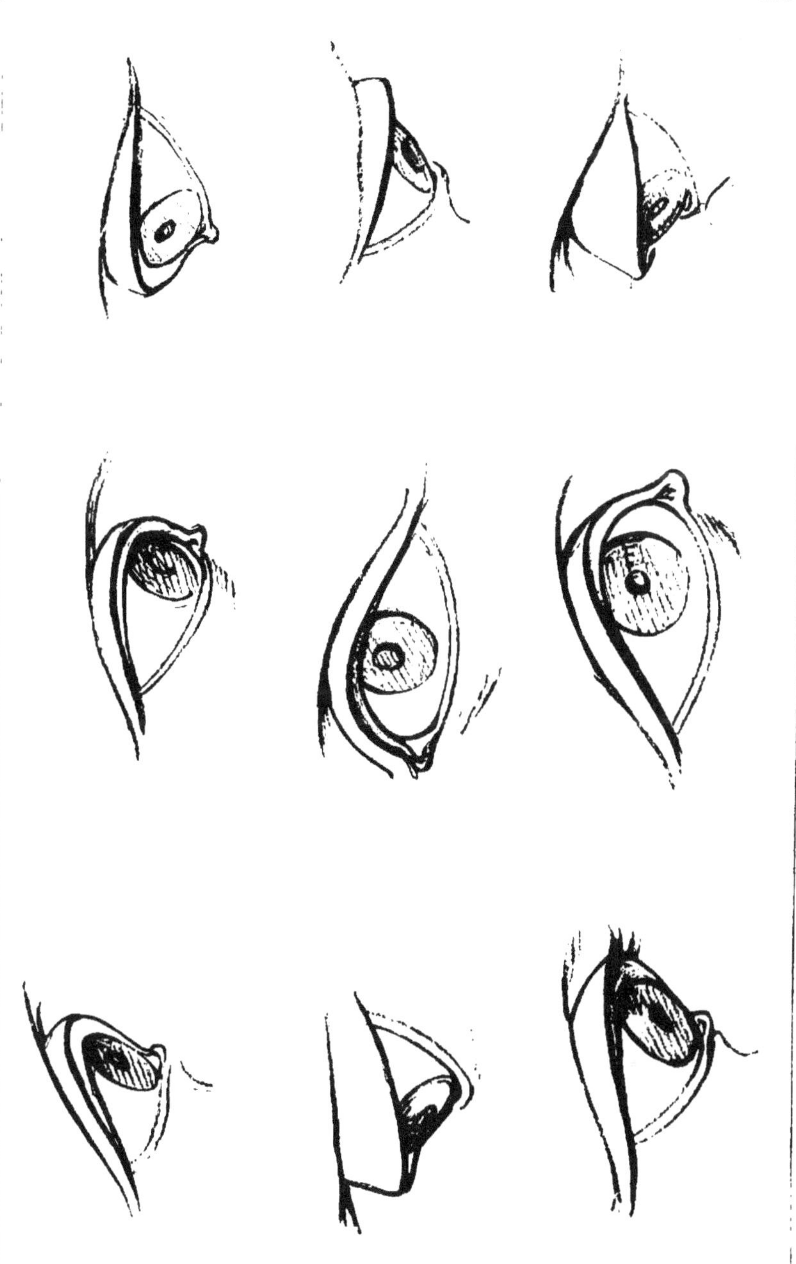

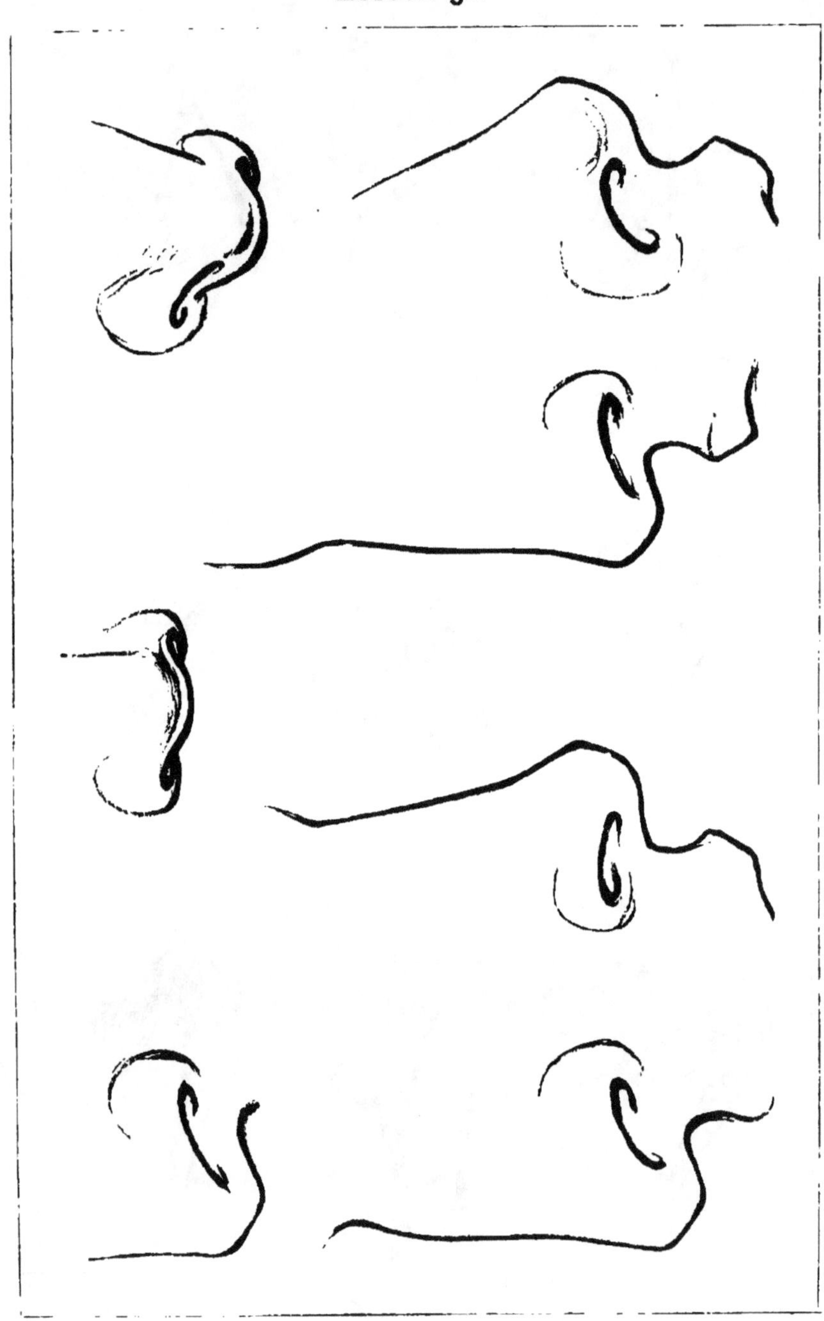

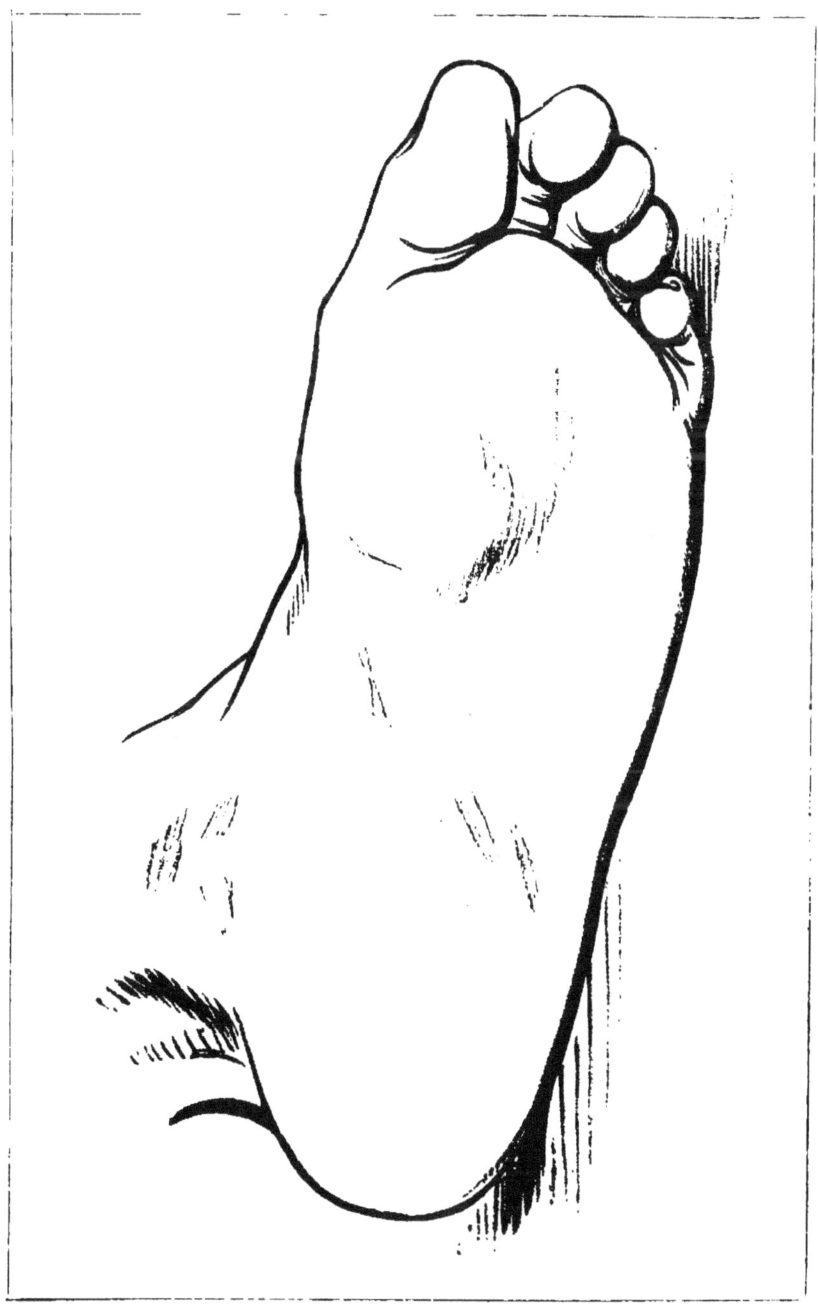

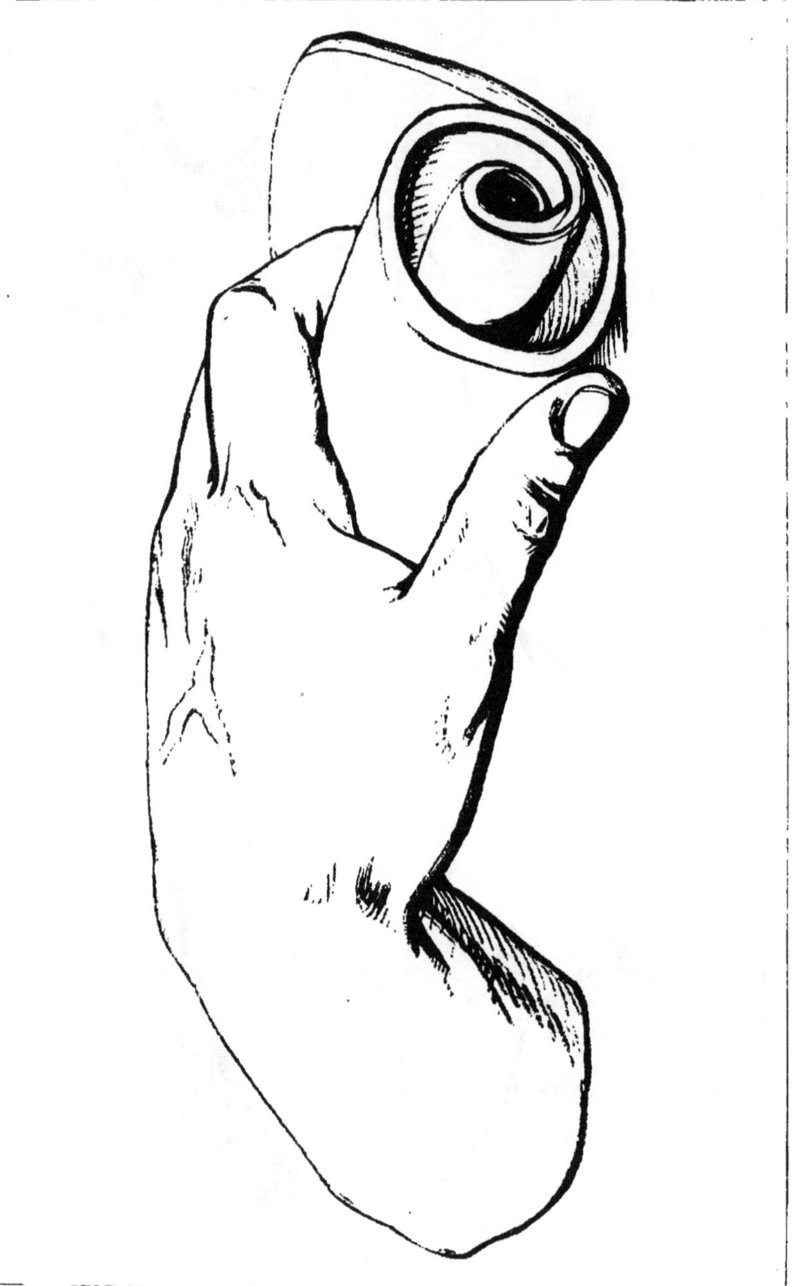

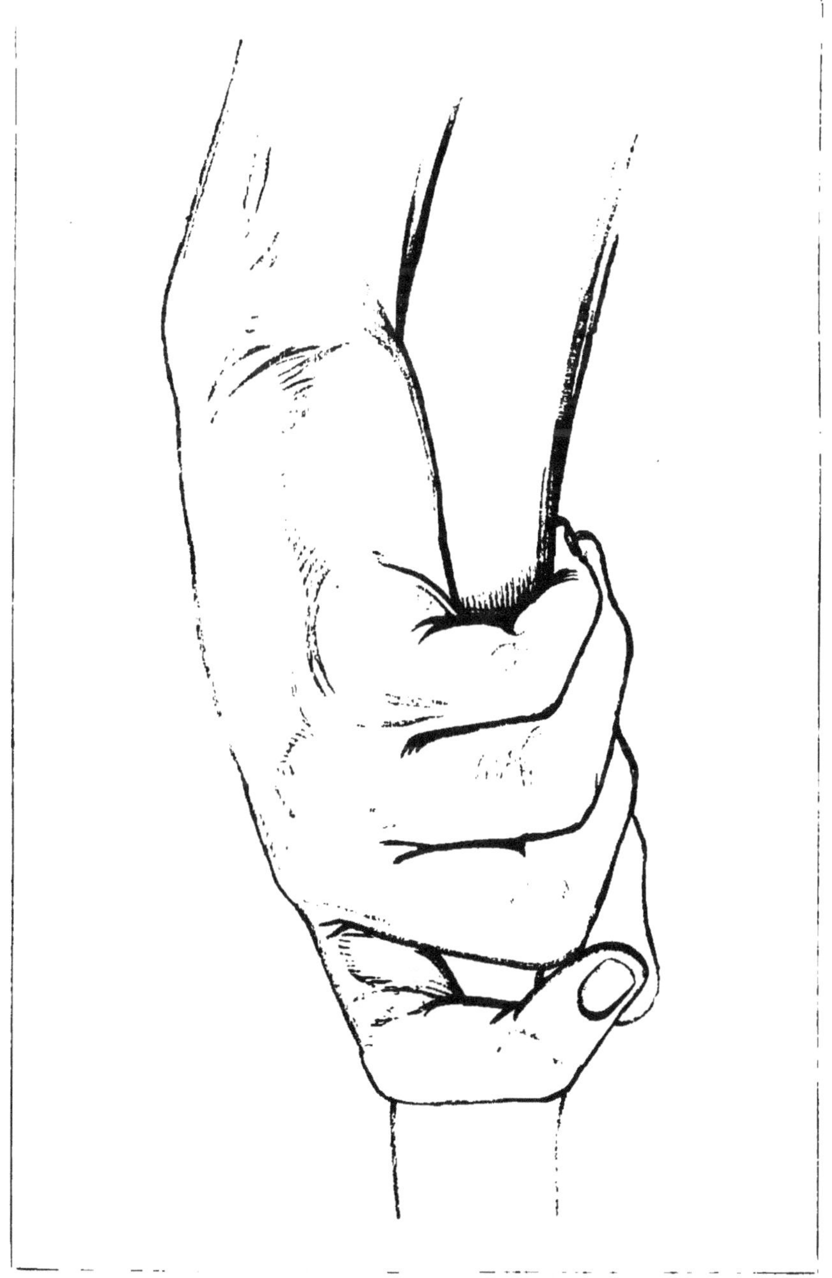

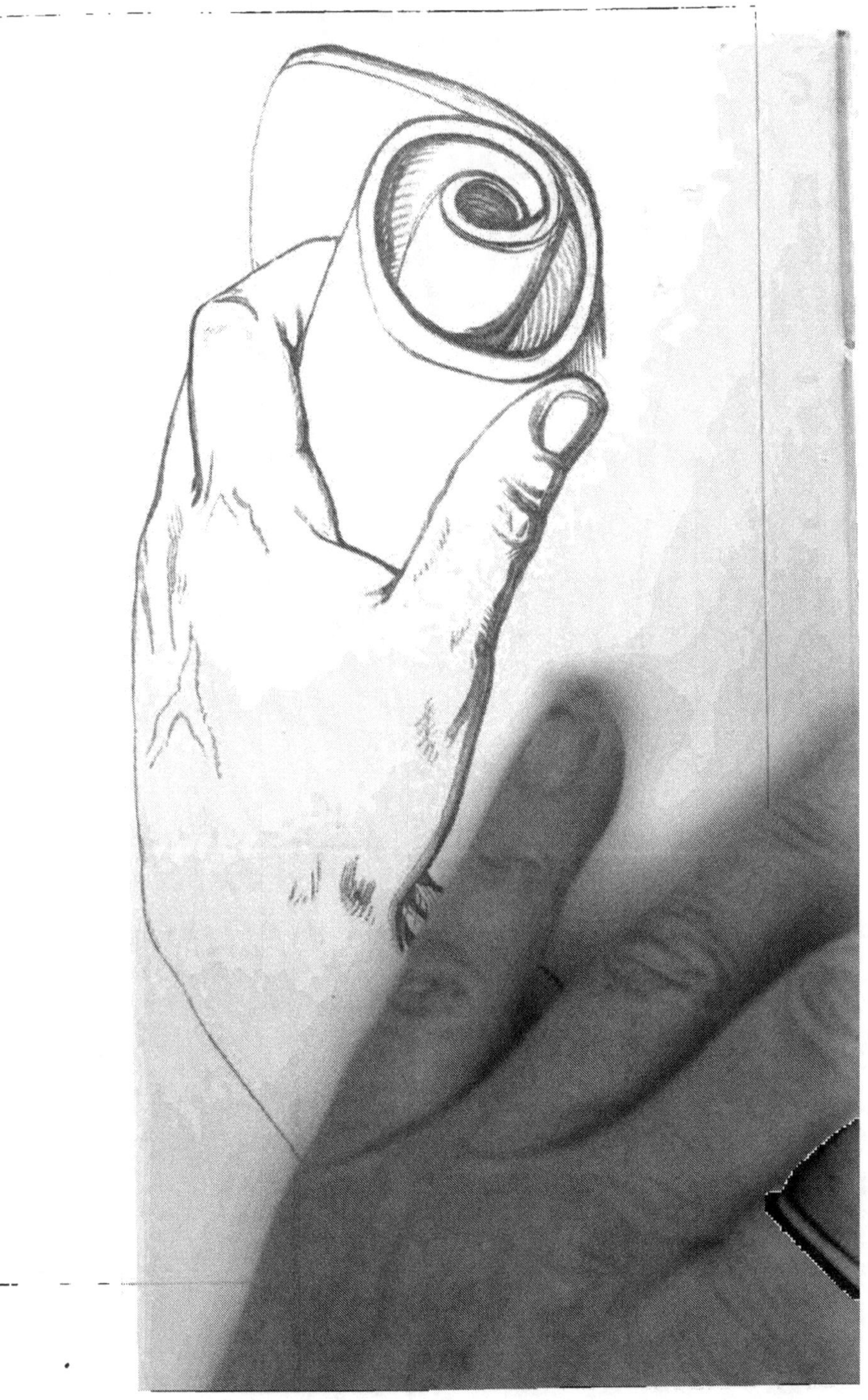

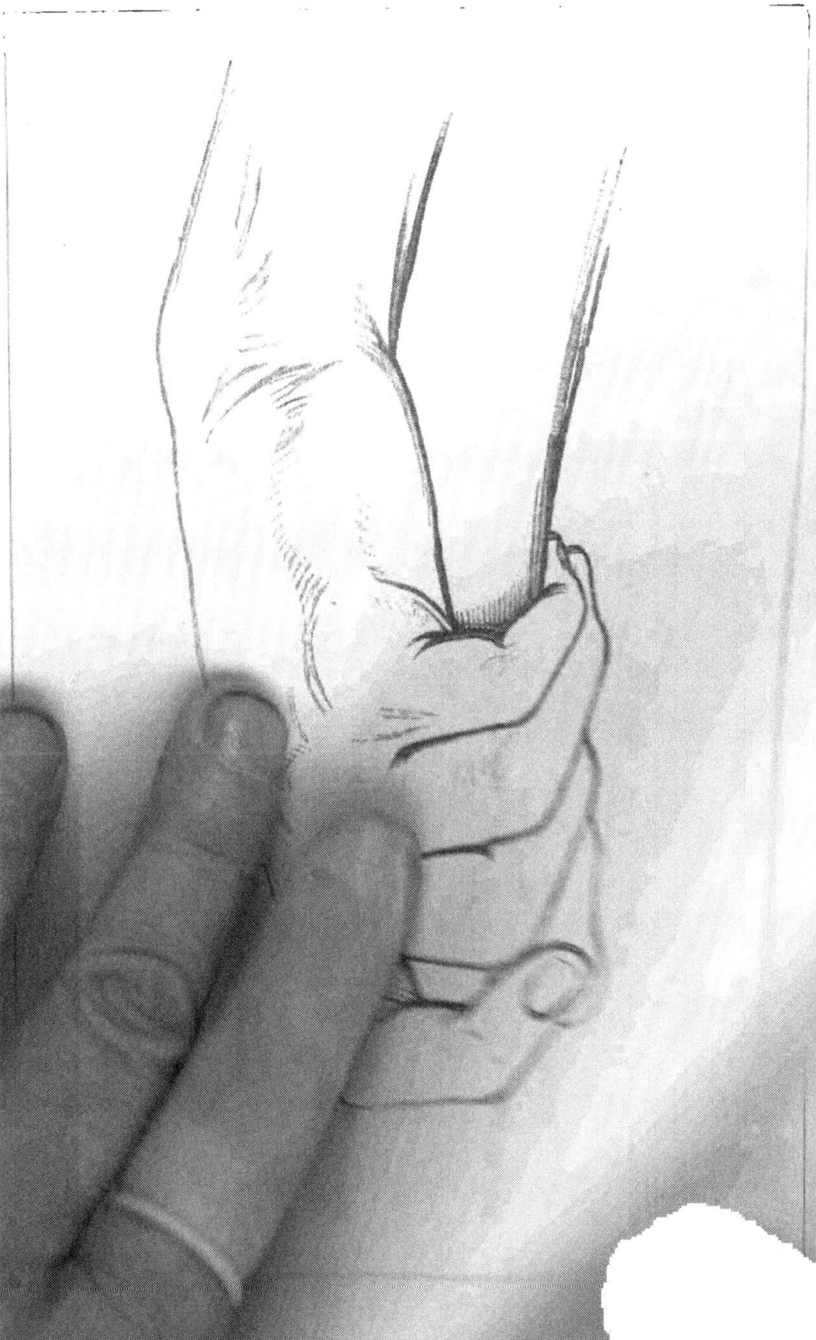

Lesson 41.

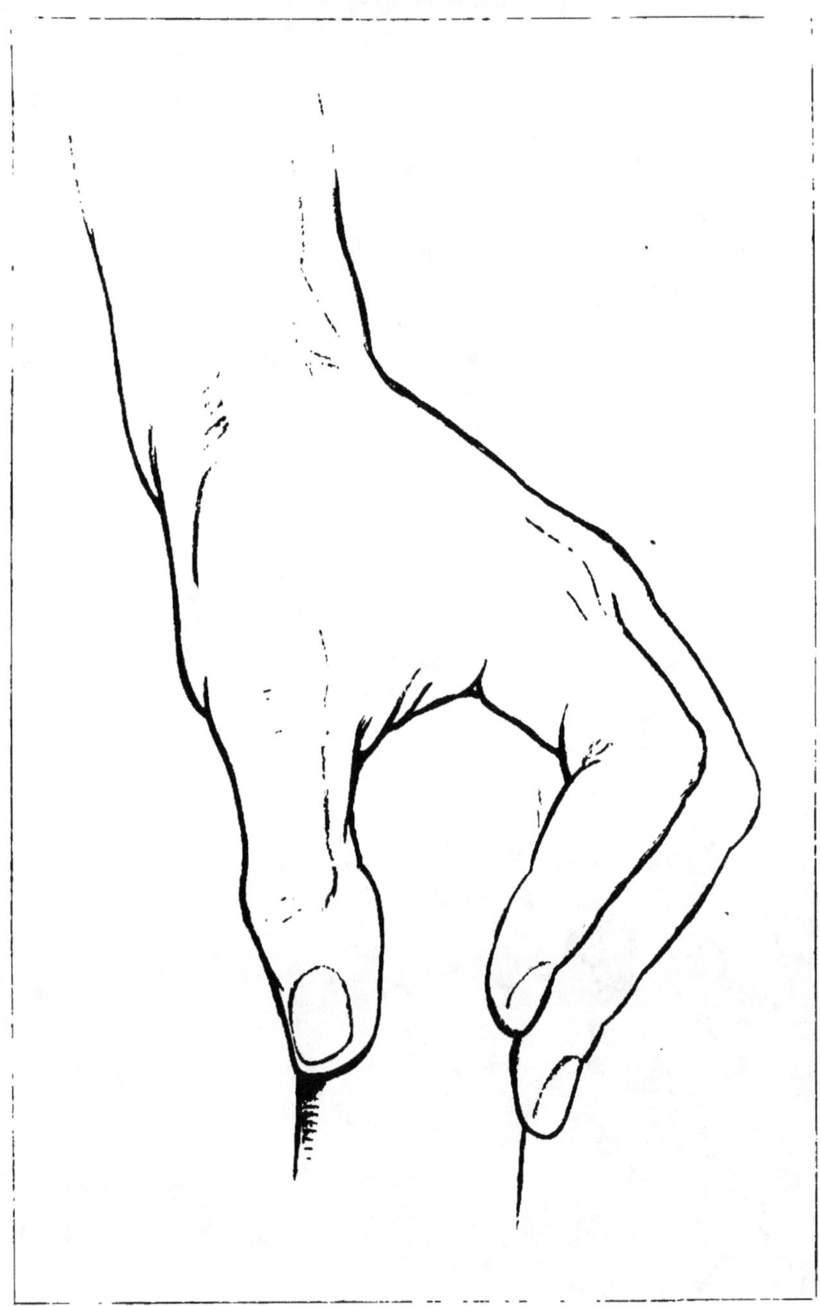

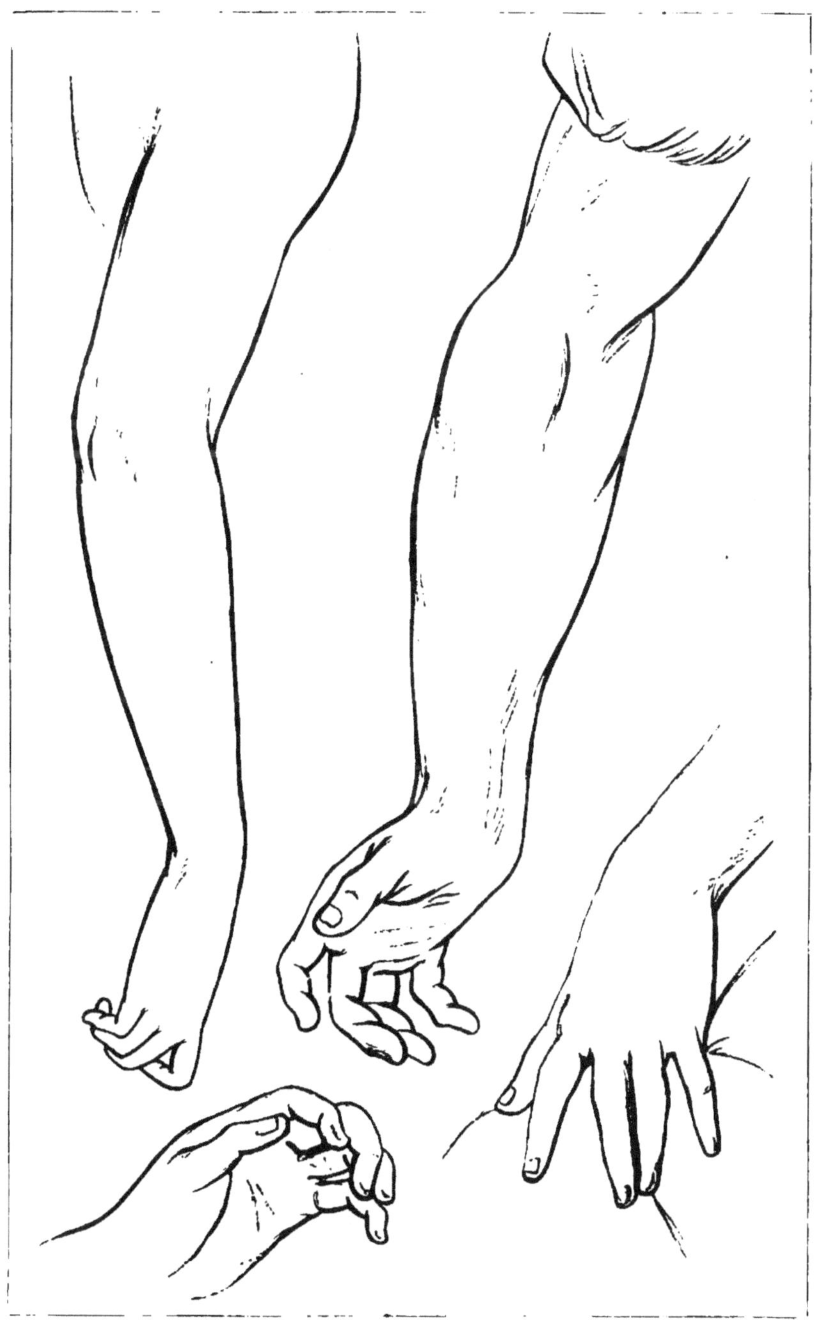

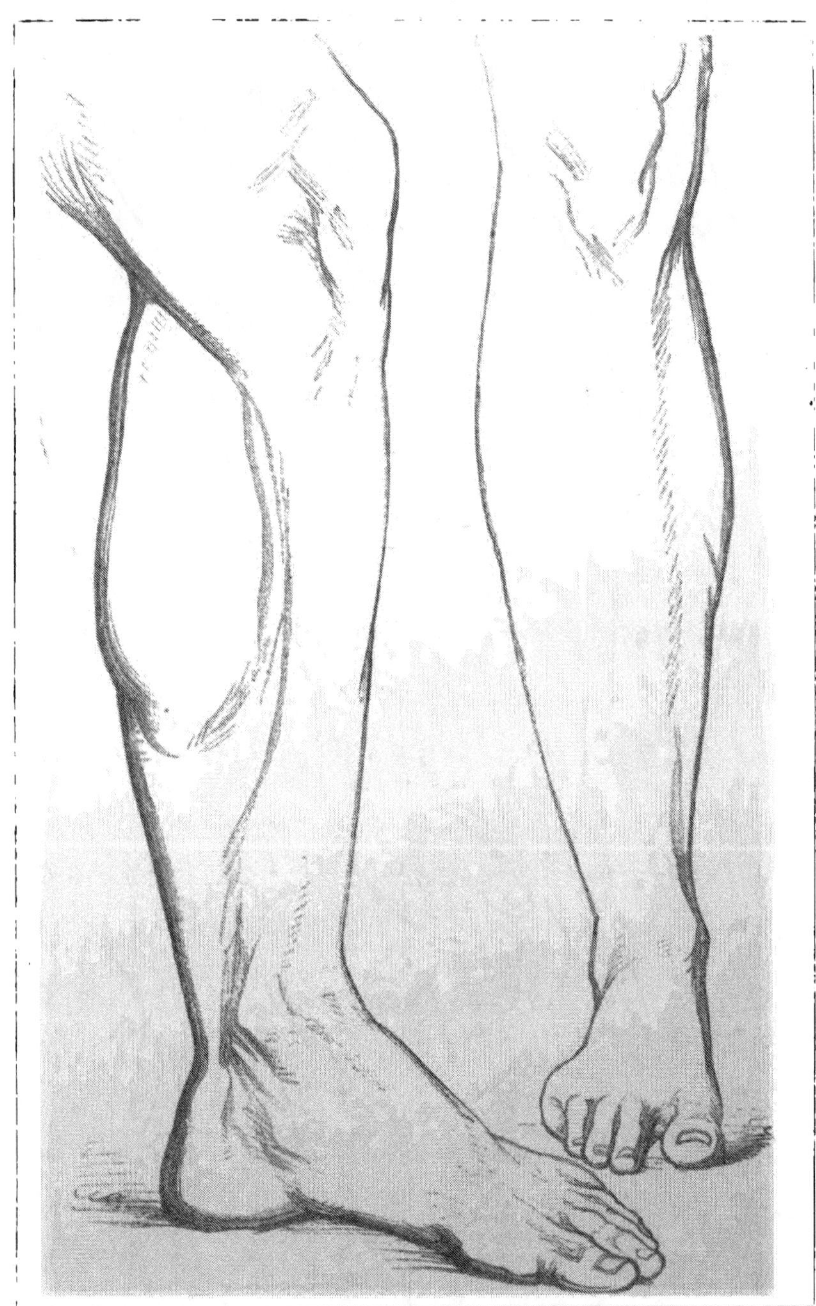

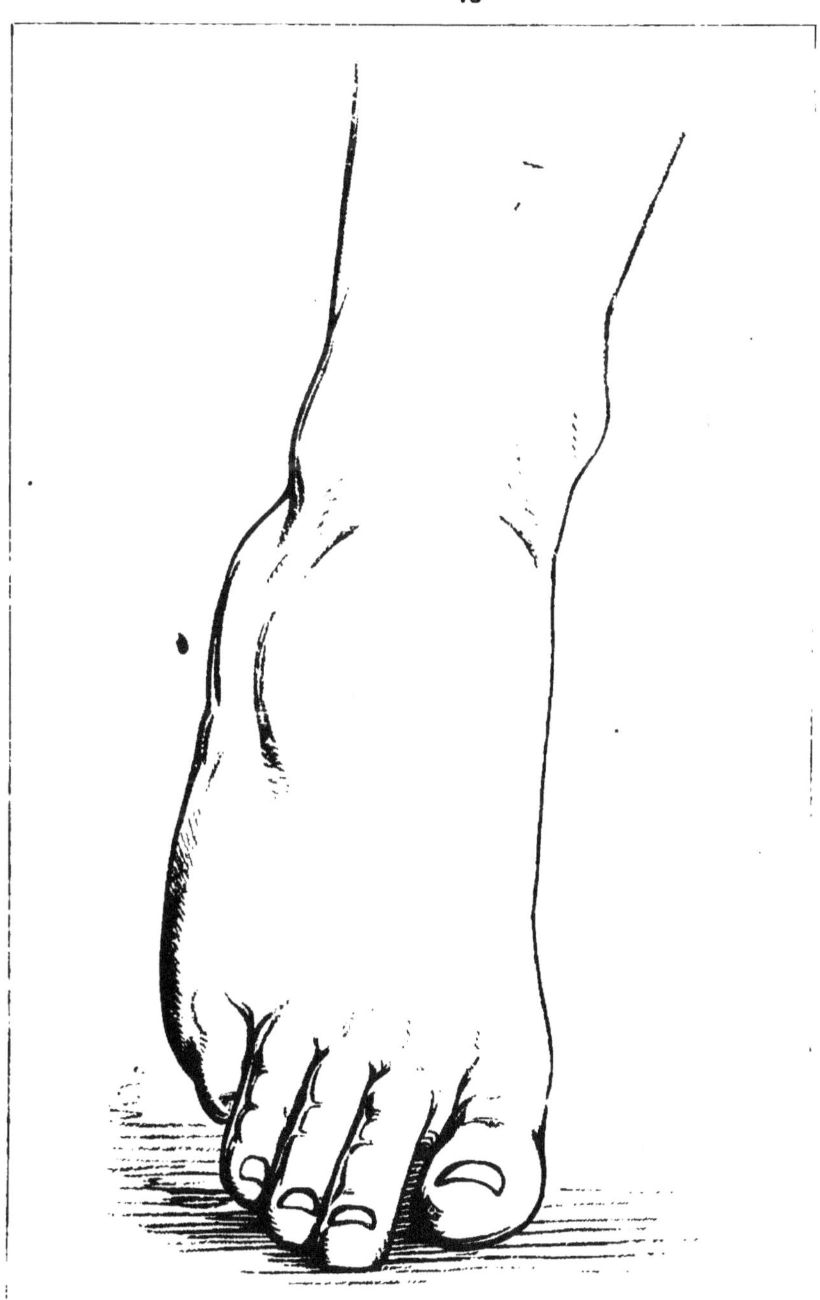

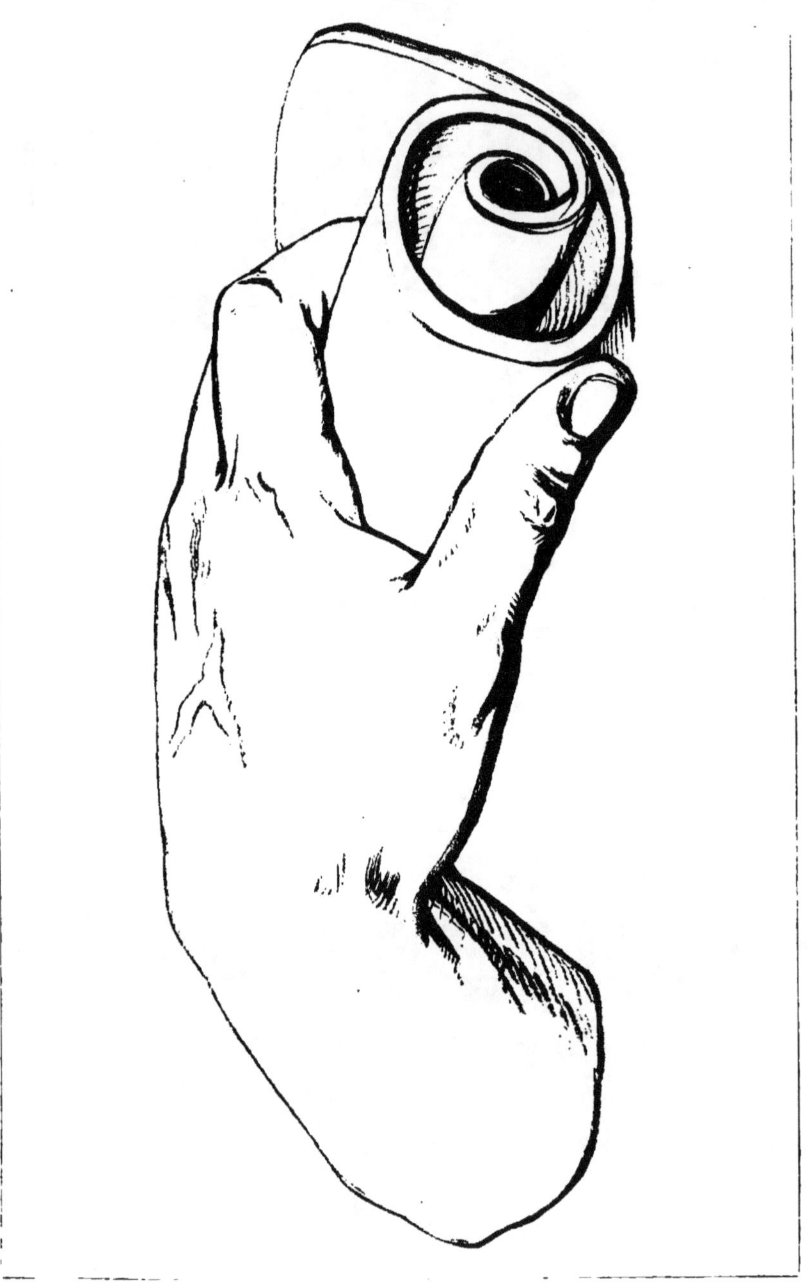

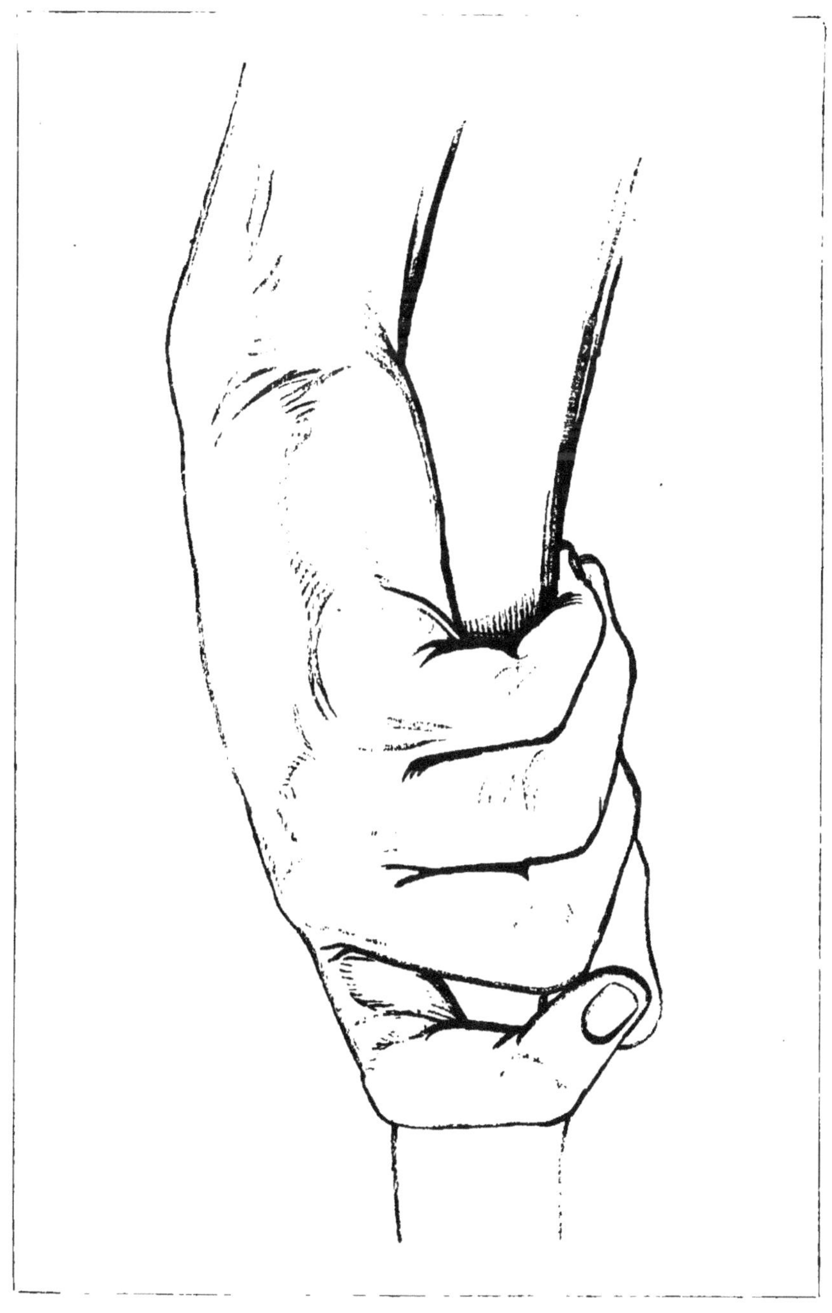

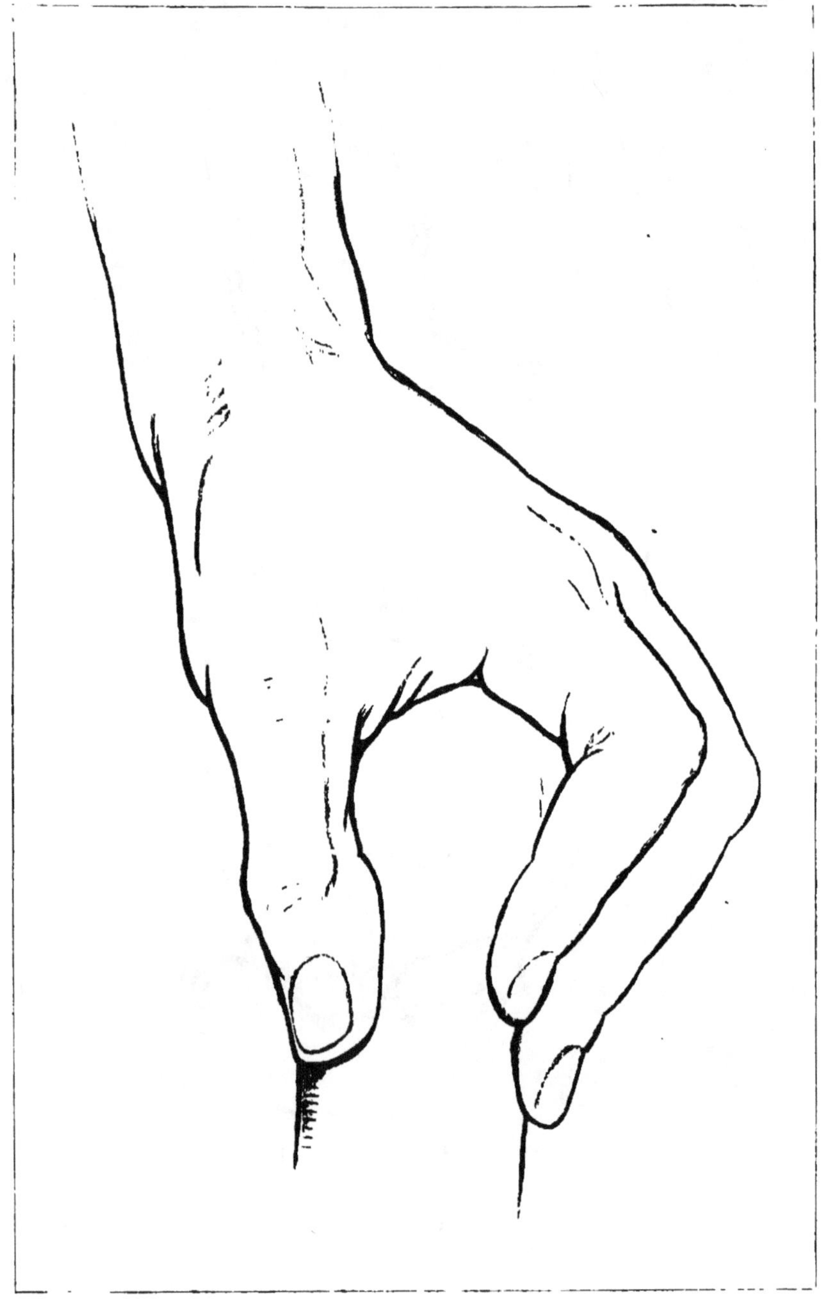

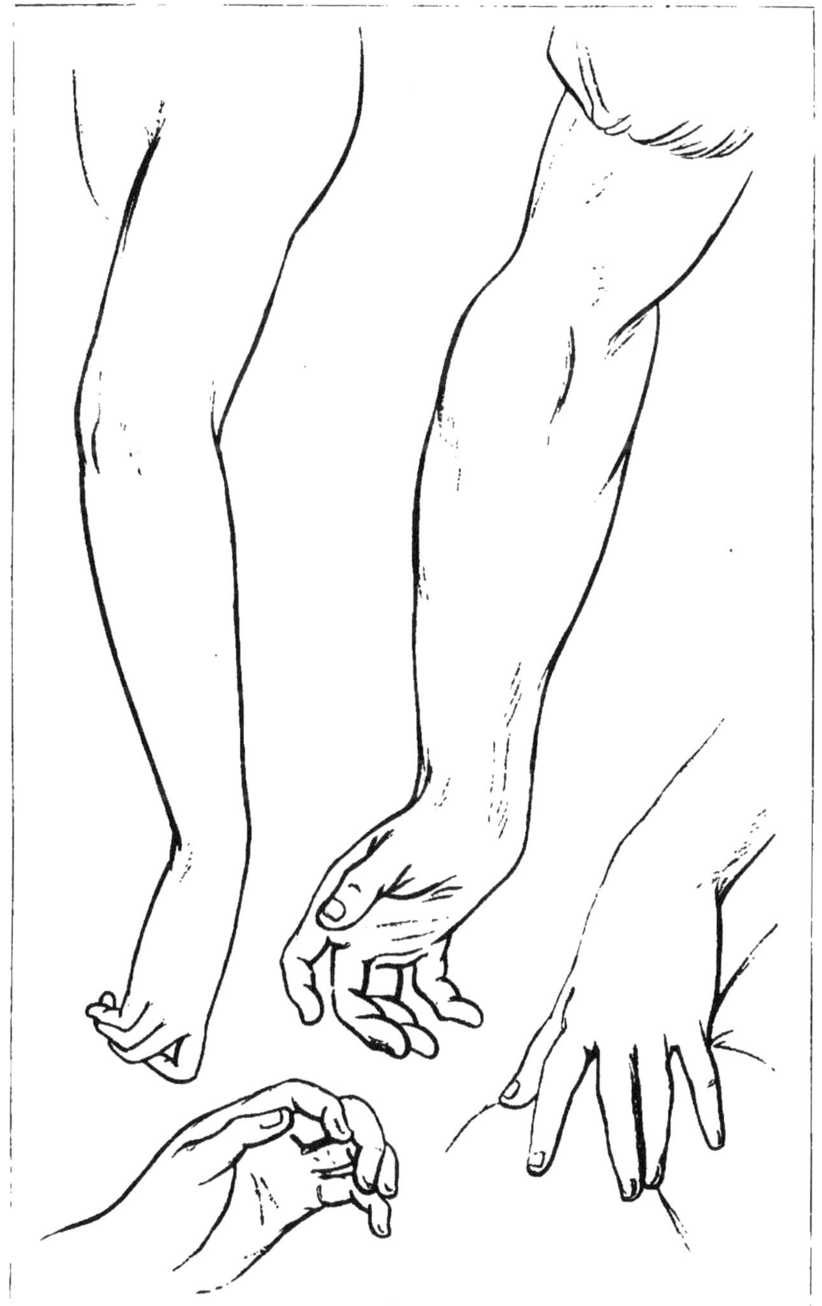

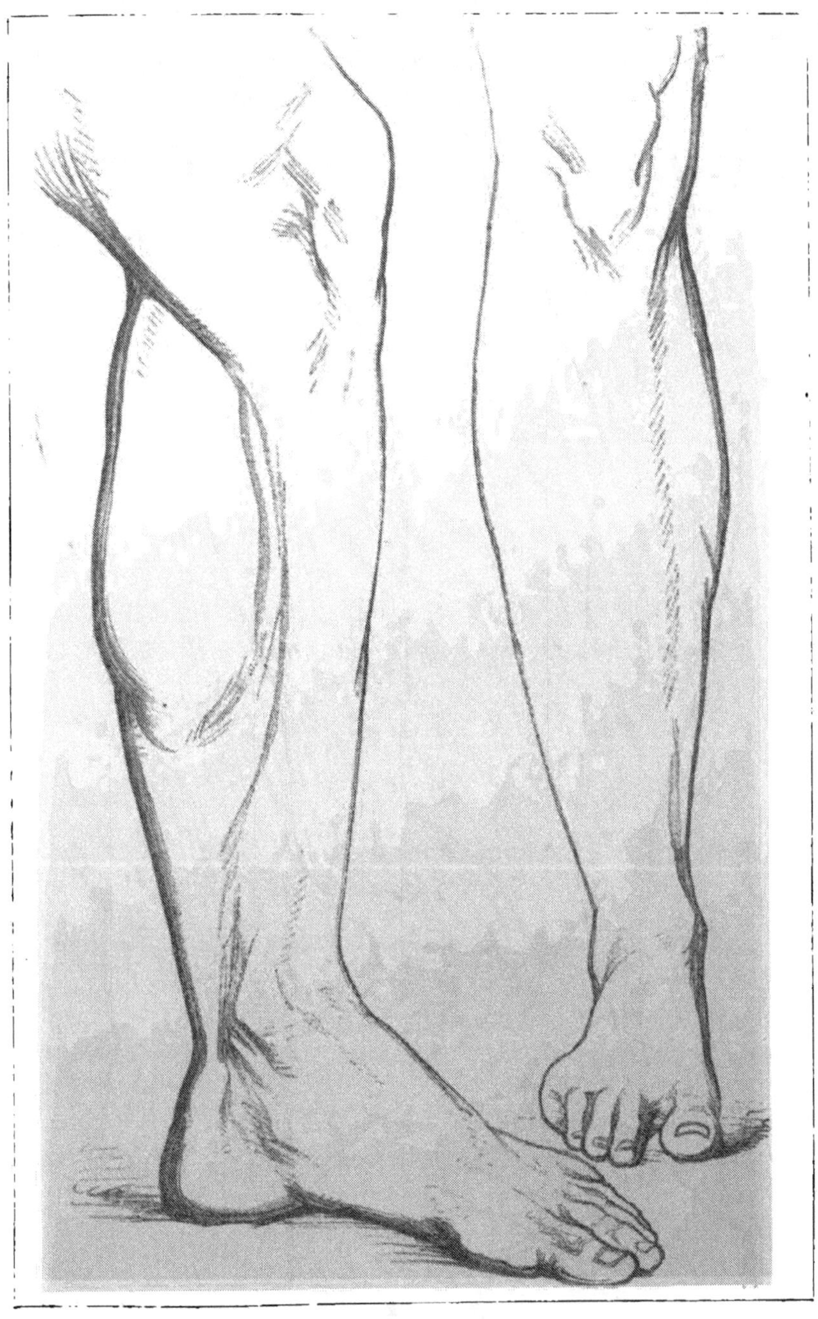

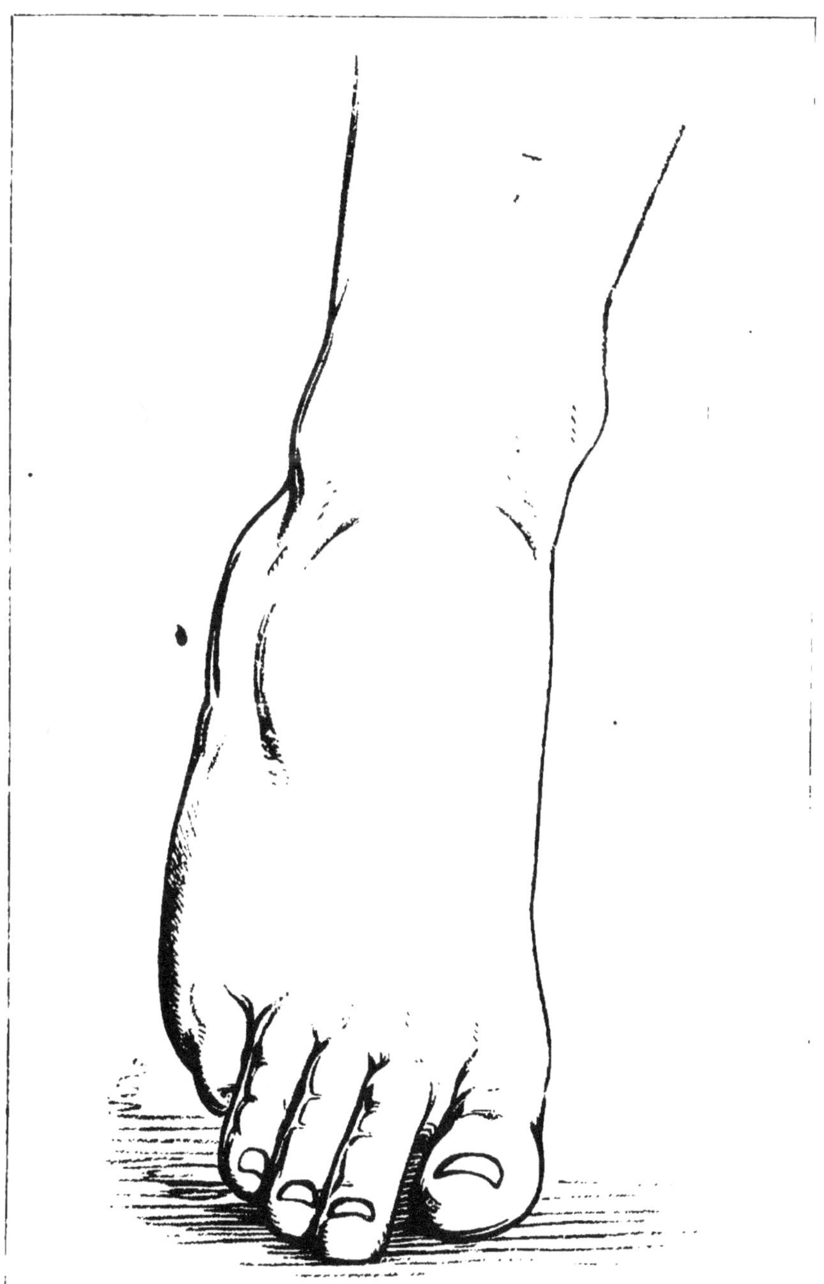

L.

Lesson 48.

LONDON:

R. CLAY, SONS, AND TAYLOR, PRINTERS,

BREAD STREET HILL.

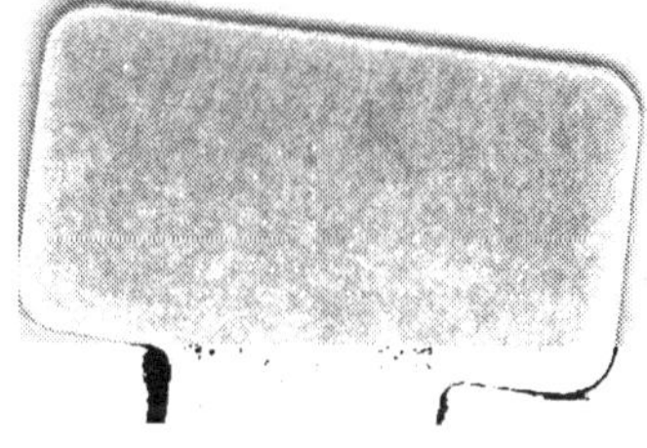